NATU[for FUN PROJECTS

Sally Hewitt

COPPER BEECH BOOKS
Brookfield, Connecticut

© Aladdin Books Ltd 2000
Produced by
Aladdin Books Ltd
28 Percy Street
London W1P 0LD

First published in the United States
in 2000 by
Copper Beech Books,
an imprint of
The Millbrook Press
2 Old New Milford Road
Brookfield, Connecticut 06804

ISBN 0-7613-0833-4

Editor: Kathy Gemmell

Consultant: Helen Taylor

Designer: Simon Morse

Photography: Roger Vlitos

Illustrators: Tony Kenyon, Stuart Squires – SGA
& Mike Atkinson

Printed in U.A.E.
All rights reserved
Cataloging-in-Publication Data
is on file in the Library of Congress.

Original design concept by David West Children's Books

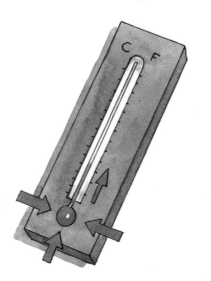

Contents

INTRODUCTION:
How to use this book
4-5

CHAPTER 1:
Weather
6-31

CHAPTER 2:
Rivers, ponds,
and seashore
32-55

CHAPTER 3:
Your backyard
56-81

CHAPTER 4:
Life cycles
82-105

CHAPTER 5:
Woods and meadows
106-129

CHAPTER 6:
All year round
130-153

GLOSSARY
154-157

INDEX
158-160

Introduction

Nature is all around us all the time. You can have fun learning about the animals and plants around where you live. Discover how to make a wind detector, look at insects skating on a pond, and see what visits your backyard when you're not there. Learn about the life cycle of a butterfly, make leaf rubbings, and build a shelter for a hibernating animal.

1

2

3

4

5

6

Look out for numbers like the ones up the side of this page. They will guide you through the step-by-step instructions for the projects and activities, making sure that you do things in the right order.

Further facts

Whenever you see this "nature spotters" sign, you will find interesting information, such as how to recognize animal footprints, to help you know and understand more.

Hints and tips

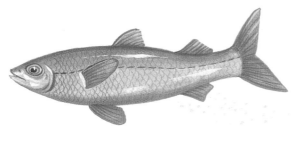

•Try to look at creatures without disturbing them. If you do move them, always return them to the place where you found them.

•When you go for a nature walk, take a waterproof coat and a sun hat, and be ready for all kinds of weather.

•Do not rub your face or eyes when working with plants or soil. Always wash your hands afterward.

Wherever you see this sign, ask an adult to help you. Never use sharp tools or go exploring by yourself.

Get an adult to help you

NEVER LOOK DIRECTLY AT THE SUN

This special warning sign shows where you have to take particular care when doing the project. For example, you should never look straight at the sun. Its powerful rays can damage your eyes and may even cause blindness.

Chapter 1:
WEATHER

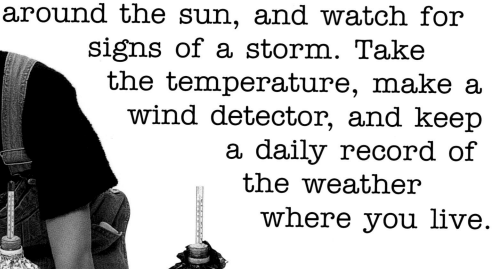

Sunshine, pouring rain, blustery wind, and snow are all different kinds of weather. You can have fun learning about the weather. Find out how the seasons change as the earth moves around the sun, and watch for signs of a storm. Take the temperature, make a wind detector, and keep a daily record of the weather where you live.

Contents

CLIMATE 8
Make your own miniclimates.

SEASONS 10
See why the seasons change.

WIND 12
Build your own wind detector.

AIR PRESSURE 14
See how air pressure affects weather.

WATER VAPOR 16
Make your own clouds.

FALLING WATER 18
See how much rain falls each day.

EVAPORATION 20
Measure how fast water disappears.

TEMPERATURE 22
Which is hotter, sun or shade?

THE SUN 24
See how colors affect temperature.

STORMS 26
Find out how far away a storm is.

POLLUTION 28
How does pollution affect weather?

RECORDING THE WEATHER 30
Build your own weather station.

Climate

Some places are hot all year round, while others are cold or rainy. The weather a place has all year is called its climate. Make your own miniclimates and see how they affect how plants grow.

Hot, cold, dry, and wet

1 Collect four plastic tubs, some paper towels, and a pack of seeds that will grow quickly, such as grass or sprouts.

2 Put paper towels in the bottom of the tubs and sprinkle seeds over them. Now put the tubs in places to copy different climates.

4 Put the last tub outside, but don't water it. Now see which of these four miniclimates is the best for growing seeds.

3 Put one of the tubs in the refrigerator. Here it will be cold, dry, and dark, just like a polar climate! Put two tubs on a warm, sunny windowsill. Water only one of these tubs and cover it with a lid.

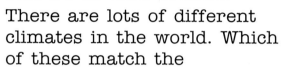

All over the world
There are lots of different climates in the world. Which of these match the miniclimates you made?

Temperate climate
Temperate climates have warm summers, cool winters, and rain during any part of the year.

Desert climate
It hardly ever rains in a desert climate. Many deserts are very hot, but some, like the North and South Poles, are very cold.

Rain forest
It rains nearly every day in a rain forest, and the air is always damp.

Seasons

The climate in some places can change from being hot one month to being cold in another. This is a change of seasons. It happens because the earth is tilted, as you will see from this project.

Tilting earth

1 You will need a friend and two balls, one for the sun and one for the earth. Paint one of them yellow to be the sun.

2 Paint a line around the middle of the other ball for the equator – an imaginary line around the earth.

3 Stick corks to the top and bottom for the poles. Now tilt the earth, and you will see that one half is closer to the sun. It will be summer here.

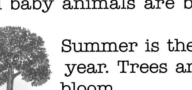 **4** Now walk around the sun. Watch the half of the earth that starts off closer to the sun now become farther away. It is now winter in this half.

The seasons

The changing seasons can bring about some dramatic changes to plants and animals.

Spring brings warmer weather after winter. Plants begin to grow, and baby animals are born.

Summer is the hottest time of the year. Trees and flowers are in full bloom.

Fall is colder. Leaves turn brown and start to fall from some trees.

Winter is the coldest season. Animals grow warm winter coats, and snow may fall.

During the summer, the arctic hare has a brown coat. In the winter, this changes to a white coat to help the hare hide in the snow.

Wind

The air around the earth is always moving, sometimes very quickly, causing storms. This moving air is called wind. Build your own detector to measure the strength of the wind.

Wind detector

1 For your wind detector, you will need a long stick, some thin string, tissue paper, writing paper, tinfoil, thin cardboard, thick cardboard, and a hole punch.

Get an adult to help you.

2 Cut a strip from each piece of paper and foil. Punch a hole in one end of each strip. Tie the strips along the stick, with the lightest at the top and the heaviest at the bottom.

Tissue paper

Writing paper

Tinfoil

Thin cardboard

Thick cardboard

3 Take your wind detector outside to see how hard the wind is blowing. A breeze will move only the tissue paper. A strong wind will move the heavier cardboard.

The Beaufort Scale

This scale is used by weather experts to measure the strength of wind.

1 No wind

2 Smoke moves

3 Leaves move

4 Branches move

5 Crests in water

6 Wind whistles

7 Trees bend

8 It's hard to walk

9 Shingles blown off

10 Trees uprooted

Air pressure

Even though you can't feel it, the air above you presses down on you all the time. This is called air pressure. Changes in air pressure usually bring changes in the weather.

Getting heavy

1 Air pressure is measured using a barometer. To make one, you will need a balloon, a glass jar, a drinking straw, a rubber band, a toothpick, scissors, and adhesive tape.

Get an adult to help you

2 Ask an adult to cut the end off the balloon and stretch it tightly over the opening of the jar. Then use the rubber band to hold the balloon firmly in place so it won't slip off.

3 Tape the toothpick to one end of the straw. Tape the other end of the straw to the stretched balloon to make a pointer.

4 Because high pressure brings good weather and low pressure bad, draw the sun at the top of a rectangle of cardboard and a cloud at the bottom.

5 Attach the cardboard behind the pointer. Watch your barometer over several days as the changes in air pressure affect the balloon, causing the pointer to rise or fall.

Pointer up

High pressure=
Good weather

Pointer down

Low pressure=
Bad weather

Barometers

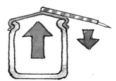

You may have a barometer at home. Its needle shows the air pressure and the kind of weather you can expect.

Compare it with your homemade barometer to see how accurate your homemade one is.

Water vapor

There are tiny droplets of water called water vapor in the air everywhere. Usually, you can't see it but when the air cools, this water vapor turns into larger drops of water and forms clouds.

Making clouds

Get an adult to help you

1 You can make a cloud in a bottle. Fill a clear plastic bottle with hot water.

2 Leave the hot water in the bottle for a few seconds. Now pour half of the water out and put an ice cube in the bottle's opening.

3 Watch as the ice cube cools the water vapor in the bottle and creates a misty cloud of water droplets.

Clouds

Clouds come in lots of shapes and form at different heights. Their shapes and positions can tell us what weather we will have.

Cirrus clouds are high and wispy. They are a warning of bad weather.

White, fluffy **cumulus** clouds can turn into storm clouds.

Cumulonimbus are dark, towering storm clouds.

Stratus are layers of low clouds and can bring rain or snow.

Falling water

The water and ice particles that make up clouds (see pages 14-15) swirl around and bump into each other, becoming bigger. If they become heavy enough, they fall to the ground as rain, hail, or snow.

Collecting rain

Get an adult to help you

1 Make a rain gauge to see how much rain falls where you live. Ask an adult to cut the top off a clear plastic bottle.

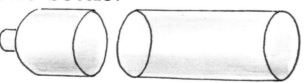

2 Turn the top of the bottle upside down and push it back inside the bottle. Tape over the sharp cut edges to make them smoother.

3 Put your rain gauge in an open place outside to catch the rain. Prop it up between four bricks to stop it from being blown over.

4 At the same time each day, pour any rain in your gauge into a measuring cup and check how much has fallen.

Snow and hail

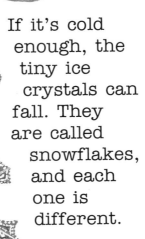

Hail is made from ice crystals in the clouds. They clump together to form small balls of ice that fall to the ground.

If it's cold enough, the tiny ice crystals can fall. They are called snowflakes, and each one is different.

Evaporation

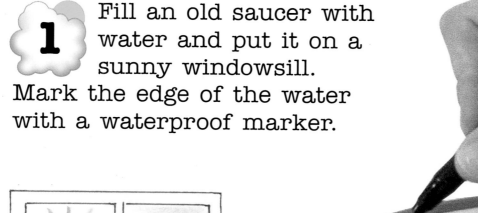

When the sun shines after a rainfall, puddles of water dry out. The water doesn't disappear, it becomes a gas called water vapor (see pages 14-15). When water does this, we call it evaporation.

Drying puddles

1 Fill an old saucer with water and put it on a sunny windowsill. Mark the edge of the water with a waterproof marker.

2 Mark the edge of the water in the saucer at the same time each day. The marks will show how quickly the water has evaporated into the air.

The water cycle

Water moves around between the land, sea, and sky in a cycle.

The sun heats up the water in oceans, rivers, lakes, and puddles and causes it to evaporate.

Water vapor in the air rises and cools. It turns into droplets of water and falls back to the ground. Rivers carry this water back to the sea, where it will evaporate again.

Water rains down

Water evaporates

Water vapor rises

Water flows downhill

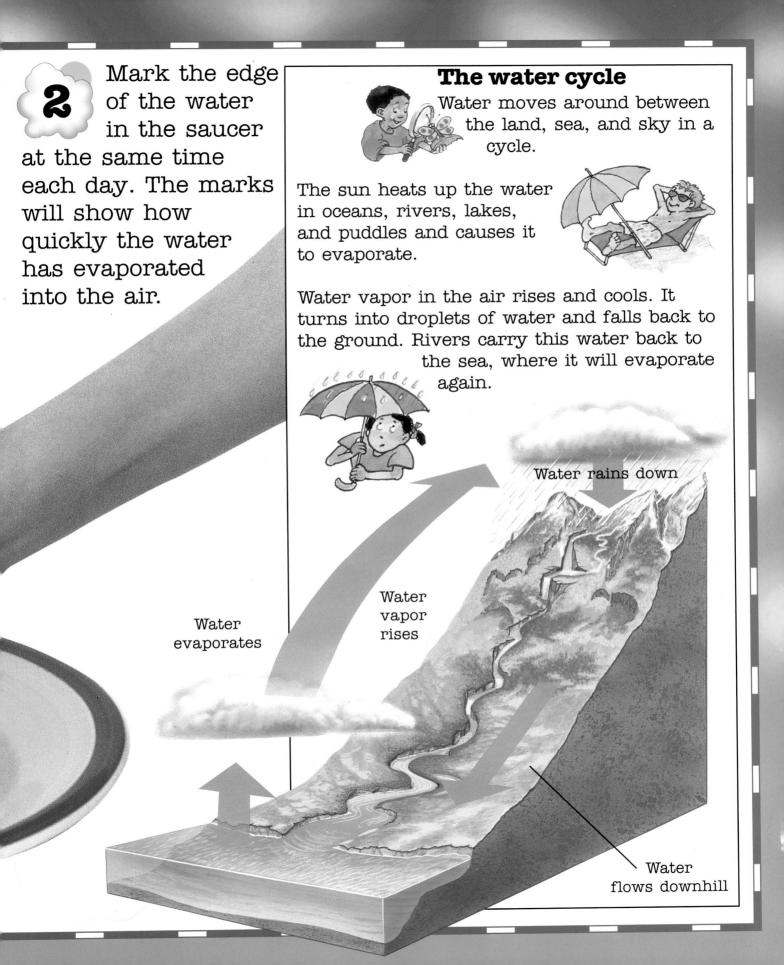

Temperature

As the weather changes, you will notice that it gets warmer or colder outside. Temperature is how hot or cold something is, and you can measure it with a thermometer.

Get an adult to help you

Sun and shade

1 You will need two thermometers. Inside their tubes is a liquid. When this liquid heats up, it expands (gets bigger) and rises up the glass tube.

2 Leave a thermometer in a sunny place. Make a note of the temperature that the liquid inside the thermometer is recording.

BE CAREFUL WITH THERMOMETERS – THE GLASS CAN BREAK!

Degrees

We measure temperature in degrees Fahrenheit, which can be written as °F.

Water boils at 212°F.

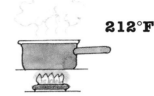

212°F

95°F outside feels very hot. Light summer clothes will help you feel cool.

95°F

Room temperature is 68°F, which feels comfortable and warm.

68°F

36°F outside feels cold. You will need to wear a warm coat and hat.

36°F

Water freezes at 32°F.

32°F

3 On the same day, leave a thermometer in a shady place. How does it feel in the shade? Is the temperature higher or lower than in the sun?

The sun

The sun's light and heat are bounced off, or reflected, by shiny things. As a result, they can be used to keep things cool. However, dark things take in heat and warm up, as you will see from this project.

Warm and cool

1 You need tinfoil, a black trash bag, two thermometers, modeling clay, adhesive tape, and two clear plastic bottles filled with cold water.

2 Cover one bottle in tinfoil and the other with the black plastic bag. Hold them in place with adhesive tape.

3 Put the thermometers into the bottles and hold them in place with modeling clay. Put the two bottles in the sun for about an hour and then check their temperature. Which bottle is warmer?

Sunglasses

Although the sun gives us heat and light, its rays are strong and can be harmful.

Sunglasses will protect your eyes from these rays in the summer.

NEVER LOOK DIRECTLY AT THE SUN!

Because snow reflects the sun, you may need sunglasses on a bright winter's day, too.

Storms

Storms are violent forms of weather, with strong winds (see pages 10-11), rain, lightning, and thunder. The best place to be during a storm is indoors. But you can still have fun experimenting with storms, even when you're inside.

Thunder and lightning

1 Thunder and lightning happen at the same time. However, because light travels faster than sound, we see the lightning before we hear the thunder. Measure the time between the flash of lightning and the crash of the thunder.

2 Figure out how far away the storm is: It takes five seconds for the sound of thunder to travel one mile. A ten second gap means the storm is two miles away.

Whirling winds

Hurricanes are giant whirling storms, hundreds of miles across. They build up over warm, wet seas and cause a lot of damage along coastal areas.

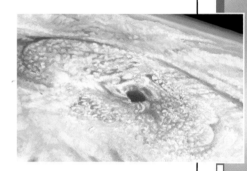

Tornadoes, or whirlwinds, are spirals of whirling air racing across land. They can pick up trucks, uproot trees, and destroy houses in their paths.

Pollution

The air around us may look clean, but it is full of dirt we can't see. Fumes from traffic, factories, and smoke all pollute the air around us, causing nasty weather, such as acid rain and smog.

Smoke gets in your eye

1 This is a way you can see pollution. Cut out one large and one small square of light colored cloth – old handkerchiefs will do.

Get an adult to help you

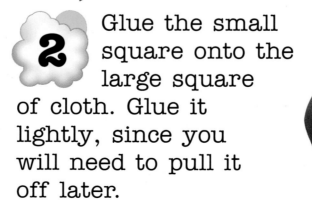

2 Glue the small square onto the large square of cloth. Glue it lightly, since you will need to pull it off later.

3 Hang the cloth up outside nearby, but not on, a busy road.

4 After at least a week, pull the small square away and see how clean the cloth is underneath! Pollution in the air has made the rest of the cloth dirty.

 ### Smog and acid rain

Pollution in the air can make rain as acidic as lemon juice! Acid rain damages trees and even wears away stone buildings and statues.

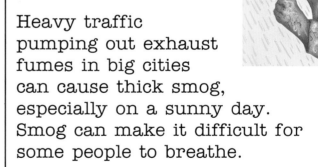

Heavy traffic pumping out exhaust fumes in big cities can cause thick smog, especially on a sunny day. Smog can make it difficult for some people to breathe.

Recording the weather

Use some of the projects in this chapter to create your own weather station. Keep a note of the measurements and see how they compare with the weather forecasts in newspapers or on television.

Keep a daily weather record

1 Hang a thermometer four feet above the ground in the shade. Read it at the same time each day.

Light wind

Light/Medium wind

Medium wind

Medium/ strong wind

Strong wind

2 Your rain gauge will tell you how wet or dry the weather has been.

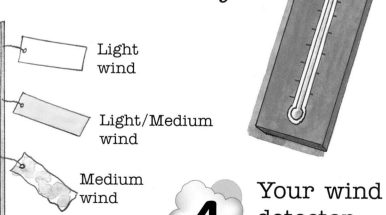

3 High or low air pressure will help you to tell if the weather is going to be dry or wet.

4 Your wind detector will let you know if it is a good day for flying a kite!

Weather maps

Weather forecasters use little pictures called symbols to make weather maps easy for us to read. Each symbol stands for a certain type of weather.

Dark storm clouds bringing thunder and lightning.

Clouds bringing rain or drizzle.

Clouds broken by patches of sunshine.

Clear skies and sunshine.

The arrow shows where the wind is coming from and how strong it is.

The number in the circle shows the temperature in degrees Fahrenheit.

Chapter 2:
RIVERS, PONDS, AND SEASHORE

Rivers, ponds, and the sea are full of all kinds of life. You can have fun learning about the things that live and grow on, by, or under the water. Go pond dipping and look out for insects skating on the water. Spot waterbirds, build a dam, and find out about the moon and the tides.

Contents

FLOWING WATER 34
See how water flows downhill.

SPEEDY RIVERS 36
Find out how fast a river flows.

POND DIPPING 38
What sort of things live in a pond?

WATER BUGS 40
Take a look at pond creepy crawlies.

BREATHING UNDERWATER 42
How can fish breathe underwater?

MAKE A POND 44
See what visits your own pond.

WATERBIRDS 46
What's so special about waterbirds?

THE TIDE 48
See what happens when the tide goes out.

SEAWEED 50
Examine this sea plant in detail.

ROCK POOLS 52
What lives in these miniworlds?

SHELLFISH 54
How many shells can you collect?

Flowing water

When water from rain, melted snow, lakes, and springs collects together, it becomes a river, carving its way through the earth as it flows downhill. See how a river can change the landscape with this project.

Make a river

1 Watch water flowing downhill by piling up stones of different sizes at one end of a plastic tray to make a hill.

2 Cover the stones with soil. Shape the soil so that you have a hill sloping down to the opposite edge of the tray.

3 Put some stones down the side of the hill on top of the soil. Now fill a jug with water and pour it on the top of the hill.

4 Watch as the water becomes a miniriver, making channels, and carrying soil downhill.

Fresh and salty water

Rainwater and the water in rivers, lakes, and springs is the water we drink and that plants need to grow. It is called freshwater, which means it is not salty.

Rivers wash salts and minerals from the land into the sea, making it salty. Saltwater is not good to drink!

Speedy rivers

Rivers are always on the move. Sometimes they drift slowly along, but at other times they can turn into a rushing torrent. This project will help you to measure the speeds of a river.

Timing sticks

1 Tie different colored string or ribbon tightly onto the end of some short sticks. Take them to a bridge over a river or stream.

DON'T STAND TOO CLOSE TO THE EDGE OF A RIVER!

2 With a friend, try to drop the sticks in the middle and at both sides of the water all at the same time.

3 Time how long it takes for the sticks to appear on the other side of the bridge. Which is the quickest?

How a river flows

Water flows swiftly along the middle of rivers and streams, where there is very little in its way. It rolls stones along and washes mud away, so the middle is usually the deepest part of a river.

Faster flow

Slower flow

Rocks and mud, as well as plants growing on the banks, all help to slow the water down. The water is usually slower and shallower at the edges of a river.

Pond dipping

Spring or summer are the best times to go pond dipping. With just a net and a plastic container, you will find all kinds of plants and animals living in every part of the pond.

DON'T LEAN TOO FAR OVER THE WATER – YOU MIGHT FALL IN!

Dippers

1 Fill a clean plastic container with pond water. Sweep your net in the water near the edge of the pond.

2 Empty the net into the container. With a magnifying glass, examine all the plants and creatures you have caught.

3 Now sweep your net nearer the middle of the pond. Have you caught different things?

Pond creatures

Here are just some of the amazing creatures that you might find living in a pond.

Sticklebacks have sharp, spiny fins along their backs.

Great pond snails have rough tongues for eating underwater plants.

Leeches hunt for fish and snails to feed on.

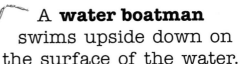

A **water boatman** swims upside down on the surface of the water.

4 Make sure you return all the living things back to the pond. Try to put them back where you found them.

Mosquito larvae hang just below the water breathing air through a tube.

Water bugs

Creatures live in every part of a pond. They live in the mud, swim in the water, and skate over the surface. Flying insects dart above the water and lay their eggs on the water plants.

Spot the creepy crawlies

1 A water spider spins its web underwater and fills it with bubbles of air. Then it lies in wait for a passing creature to catch and eat.

Dragonfly

Water spider

2 A dragonfly darts above the water catching insects with its legs. It has see-through wings and a shiny, colorful body.

3 A whirligig beetle whirls around on the water as it hunts for food.

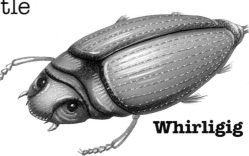

Whirligig

Gnat

4 Female gnats suck a tiny amount of blood for a meal from animals or people. They lay their eggs on the water.

5 A pond skater jumps and slides over the skin of the water without breaking it.

Pond skater

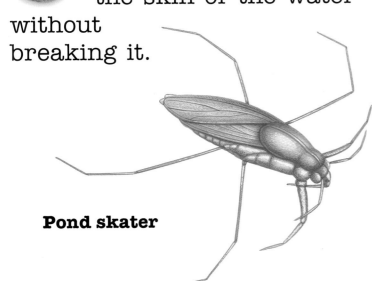

Water skin

Fill a glass to the brim with water so that it is almost overflowing. You can see that the water bulges over the top of the glass as if it has a thin skin.

Pollution in the water breaks up this skin. As a result, creatures like pond skaters that live on the surface cannot live in polluted ponds.

Breathing underwater

Water creatures need to breathe oxygen to live. Some come up to the surface for air, but others stay underwater and breathe the oxygen that is mixed into the water. This project shows you how water plants give off oxygen into the water.

Weedy air

1 You will need pondweed, a funnel, a plastic bottle of water, three lumps of modeling clay, and a see-through container.

2 Put the weed and clay in the bottom of the container and fill with water. Place the funnel on the lumps of clay so that it sits over the pondweed.

3 Carefully place the bottle of water upside down over the funnel. Watch how bubbles of oxygen gradually come from the weed and fill the bottle.

Breathing underwater

Fish do not have lungs; they breathe through special organs called gills. These lie just behind the eyes of a fish.

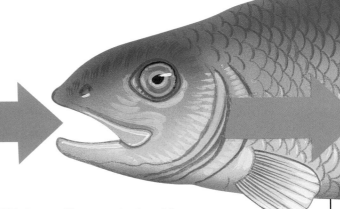

Water flows into the fish's mouth and passes over the gills. Oxygen in the water is taken into the fish's blood as it flows over its gills.

Lungfish have lungs and gills so that they can breathe both in and out of water. If the water they live in dries up, they can hide in the mud until it rains again.

Make a pond

You have already seen some of the plants and animals that live in ponds. Now build one yourself and see if you can attract some of this wildlife to your own pond.

1 You will need a flat tray, gravel, soil, large stones, and some water plants, such as pondweed.

2 Cover the bottom of the tray with gravel and some soil. Use a big stone to make an island in the middle.

3 Carefully fill the tray with water. Try to use rainwater, as it is best for a pond.

4 Add the plants, fixing them with stones and soil. Or you can plant them in the water in little pots.

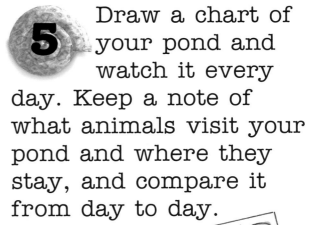

5 Draw a chart of your pond and watch it every day. Keep a note of what animals visit your pond and where they stay, and compare it from day to day.

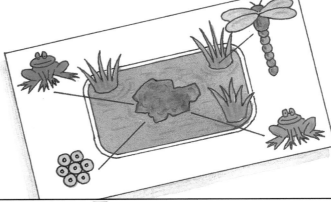

Frogs

Frogs spend the first part of their lives as tadpoles living underwater. Grown–up frogs live in water and on land.

Frogs lay eggs called frog spawn in the water.

 Tadpoles hatch from the eggs and swim underwater.

Tadpoles lose their tails, grow legs, and become little frogs.

Waterbirds

Waterbirds live on rivers, ponds, and the seashore. Watch some waterbirds carefully. In what ways are they like this duck? How are they different?

BE CAREFUL NOT TO SCARE WATERBIRDS!

1 This duck has a flat bill. It uses its bill to filter out seeds, insects, and snails from the water to eat.

2 It also uses its bill to spread oil through its feathers to make them waterproof. Drops of water roll easily off the oil.

Shapes and sizes

Here are some examples of the different types of waterbirds.

Pelican

A pelican uses its long, strong bill with a pouch like a fishing net to scoop fish out of the water.

Kingfisher

A kingfisher sits on a branch and spots fish to catch in its pointed beak in the water below.

Black-headed gull

A black-headed gull has a hooked bill for catching slippery fish and tearing at food.

Spoonbill

A spoonbill has long, thin legs. It uses these to wade through shallow water, while it picks up food from the bottom with its spoon-shaped bill.

3 Skin stretched between its three toes turn a duck's feet into a kind of paddle. Many waterbirds have webbed feet like these.

The tide

Driftwood

When you go to the beach, you may notice that the edge of the sea moves backward and forward each day. This is called the tide.

BE AWARE OF FAST OR STRONG TIDES

Shells

Beachcombing

1 When the sea is at low tide, you will see a mark on the sand where the high tide was. Measure the distance between the low tide and the high tide by pacing it out.

Seaweed

2 Look at the part of the beach you can only see when the tide is low. You should see small piles of sand made by worms as well as bird tracks.

3 As the sea pulls away from the shore, it leaves all kinds of things behind, such as seaweed and bits of pottery. Make a note of some of the things you find by the sea at low tide.

Pottery

Pebbles

High and low tide

The tides are actually caused by the sun and the moon.

Gravity is the force that keeps your feet on the ground and causes things to fall to the ground.

The gravity of the sun and the moon pulls the water in the sea, causing tides.

Seaweed

Seaweeds can be found all along the seashore. They do not have roots like plants that grow on land but have special roots, called holdfasts, that grip onto rocks. This project shows you a good way to study seaweed in close-up.

Floating seaweed

1 Collect some seaweed to take home. Find a see-through vase or jar. Put in the seaweed and use a stone to hold it on the bottom. Now add water.

2 Look at the shape of seaweed when it is held up by water. See how it goes limp and loses its shape out of water.

Types of seaweed

There are three types of seaweed that you can find washed up on the seashore – red, brown, and green.

Carrageen is a red seaweed. You might find some growing in a rock pool.

Bladder wrack is a brown seaweed. It has little pockets of air to help it float upright in the water.

Sea lettuce is a green seaweed that looks like the lettuce leaves we eat.

Rock pools

As the tide goes out it leaves behind pools of water among the rocks. Rock pools are places where you can find creatures and plants hiding. Make your own special viewer to see this underwater world clearly.

TAKE CARE ON THE SLIPPERY ROCKS AROUND ROCK POOLS!

Underwater viewer

1 Cut the top and bottom off a plastic bottle and tape over the rough edges to make your underwater viewer.

Get an adult to help you

2 Pull plastic wrap tightly over one end. Put a rubber band around the plastic wrap to stop it from slipping off your viewer.

Life in a rock pool

All kinds of sea creatures live together in a rock pool. Below are just some of the animals you might find. Keep still and try to keep your shadow off the pool or you might scare the creatures into hiding.

Make a note of what you see and where you see it. Then compare your chart the next day.

Mussel

Sea anemone

Shrimp

Shore crab

Goby

Starfish

Dog whelk

Sea urchin

3 Put the end covered with plastic wrap into the water and look through the viewer. You should be able to see the bottom of the rock pool.

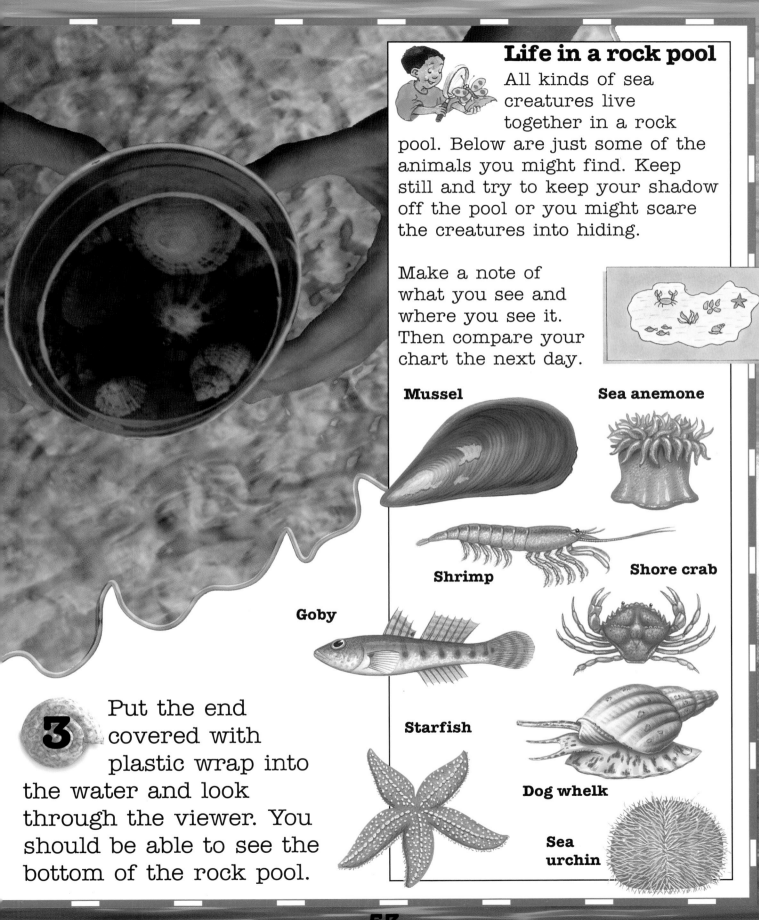

Shellfish

Shellfish have soft bodies, so they grow a tough shell to protect them. There are many different types of shellfish. Make a collection of shells you find on the beach and sort them into groups like these.

DON'T TAKE SHELLS WITH LIVE CREATURES INSIDE!

Mussels

Scallops

Limpets

Razor clams

4 Scallops, mussels, and razor clams live in shells with hinges. These open up to let the creature feed.

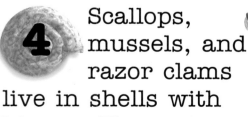

3 Limpets have a single shell to hide under while they cling tightly to a rock.

Collecting shells

1 Arrange your shells into groups depending on each shell's size and shape.

2 These spiral-shaped shells used to be the homes of snail-like animals such as whelks.

Spiral shells

Useful shells

Shellfish have developed some amazing features to feed or protect themselves from creatures who want to eat them.

A **barnacle** waves its legs through a small hole in the top of its shell. It uses these to catch any food which may be floating past.

A **limpet** moves slowly over a rock, scraping off food with its teeth-filled mouth.

A **scallop** escapes from a hungry starfish by flapping its shells open and shut and jet–propelling itself along.

Chapter 3:
YOUR BACKYARD

Look closely and you will find many interesting things in your backyard. Have fun learning about creatures and where to find  them. Make a worm garden and watch worms at work in the soil. Plot an ant map and attract birds with a cake. Discover how to find out who visits the yard when you're not there.

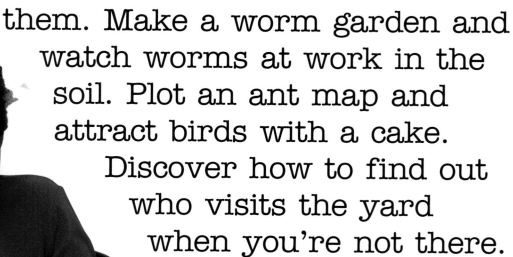

Contents

SOIL **58**
Find out how soil is formed.

ROTTING GARBAGE **60**
See how some garbage disappears.

SEEDS **62**
Grow your own garden.

GREEN GRASS **64**
Find out why grass is green.

PLANTS **66**
Watch plants drink.

FLOWERS **68**
Discover different flower parts.

FEEDING BIRDS **70**
Make a bird cake.

FOOTPRINTS **72**
Find out who visits your backyard.

INSECT VISITORS **74**
Where do insects live?

MINIBEASTS **76**
Build a trap and see what crawls out.

ANTS **78**
Trace ant paths with sugary bread.

WORMS **80**
Make your own worm garden.

Soil

Soil is a very important part of your backyard. It is full of the minerals and water that plants need for growth. Moles, worms, and all kinds of tiny creatures make it their home.

Soil settling

1 Find out what makes up the soil in your backyard. Dig up some soil from the edge of a flower bed and put it in a bucket.

2 Shake some soil in a sieve over the bucket. Sort what is left behind onto some paper. You may find stones, bits of plants, or even creatures that live in the soil.

3 Now put some soil into a screw-top jar. Fill the jar nearly to the top with water and screw on the lid.

4 Shake the soil and water together, then leave the jar to stand.

5 Carefully look at the jar without disturbing it. The soil will settle into layers in the water.

Soil layers

Soil is a mixture of dead plants and animals and tiny pieces of broken-down rock. Different kinds of rock will make sandy, chalky, or sticky clay soil.

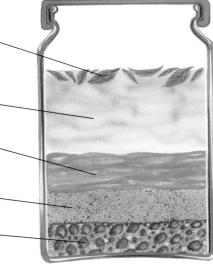

Bits of plants

Muddy water

Clay or chalk

Sand

Gravel and stones

Rotting garbage

Dead plants and animals that rot down into the soil help to make it rich and good for new plants to grow in. Not everything rots down quickly. Some garbage stays around for a very long time.

Bags of garbage

1 See what kind of garbage rots away, and what doesn't. Don't throw away banana skins, apple cores, tissues, cans, or potato chip bags - bury them!

NEVER TAKE GARBAGE FROM THE CAN

2 Put some soil into clear plastic bags. Push one piece of garbage into the soil in each bag and seal it.

3 Check the bags every few days, but don't open them. You will see that apple cores rot quickly, but banana skins take a long time. Garbage made of plastic doesn't rot at all.

Natural rotters

There are many different plants and animals that get to work right away on natural garbage like leaves, logs, or dead creatures. They are called decomposers.

Fungi are not really plants. They grow and feed on dead wood.

Lichens grow on stone and wood and gradually break them down.

Worms pull leaves and bits of dead plant down into the soil and eat them.

Maggots that hatch from housefly eggs eat the bodies of dead creatures.

Woodlice live in dark, damp places and feed on leaves and wood.

Seeds

Gardeners look after the plants and flowers they want to grow in their yards, and spend a lot of time pulling up weeds that they didn't plant. You can discover what seeds are hiding in the soil, waiting to grow.

Soil gardens

1 Dig up some soil from two different places in the yard, perhaps from under a tree and by a fence. Put the soil from each place in its own plastic tray and label where it came from.

2 Water both trays every other day. After a while, you will see shoots beginning to push up through the soil even though you didn't plant any seeds.

3 Some shoots may become grass or weeds. A seed from a tree may one day grow into a young tree. A rose tree may even grow from a rose hip dropped by a bird.

Spreading seeds

Plants have various ways of spreading their seeds to give them a good chance to grow into new, strong plants.

Birds eat juicy fruits, such as cherries. The seeds or pits inside them fall to the ground in the birds' droppings.

Horse chestnut seeds are heavy and fall straight to to the ground. Look for them under a horse chestnut tree.

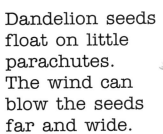

Dandelion seeds float on little parachutes. The wind can blow the seeds far and wide.

Green grass

Grass in the countryside is food for animals and it can be like a soft, green carpet in the yard. Grass has another job to do, too.

Grass roots hold soil in place in the wind and the rain. Different kinds of grass grow in different soils.

In the dark

1 This project will show you that sunlight is what makes grass green. Find a corner of your lawn.

2 Cover a patch of grass, near the edge of the lawn, with a thick piece of cardboard. Put a stone on it to stop it blowing away.

3 Lift up the cardboard after two weeks and see what has happened to the grass. When kept in the dark, grass will turn pale green or yellow and begin to die.

Using sunlight

Like grass, other plants also need sunlight to grow and survive. Plants make their own food using sunlight. This is called photosynthesis.

Photosynthesis

Plants need sunlight to make food using the green color in their leaves, called chlorophyll.

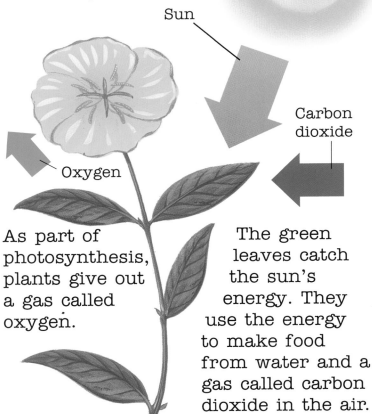

Sun

Carbon dioxide

Oxygen

As part of photosynthesis, plants give out a gas called oxygen.

The green leaves catch the sun's energy. They use the energy to make food from water and a gas called carbon dioxide in the air.

Without sunlight, plants cannot make food and they will die.

Plants

We all have veins to carry blood around our bodies. Plants have veins, too. They carry the water and mineral a plant needs to grow to every part of the plant. Watch how water moves up the stem and into the leaves of a celery stalk.

Drinking water

1 For this project you will need a jar of water, some blue food coloring, and a celery stalk with leaves.

2 Mix the water and blue food coloring together in the jar and put the celery stalk in it. Leave the jar near a window for a few hours.

3 The blue water will slowly rise up the veins in the stalk, then into the leaves, turning them blue.

Get an adult to help you

4 Now slice the stalk across the middle. You will be able to see that the veins in the celery have been stained blue.

Roots

Roots grow downward into the soil to hold the plant in place. They have tiny hairs to suck up the water and minerals that a plant needs from the soil. Water goes into the roots, then up the stem into the leaves, then out into the air.

Carrots and potatoes are swollen roots that store food for the plants.

Water in the soil

Flowers

A plant starts life as a tiny egg. Flowers are the parts of a plant where eggs that become seeds are made. The seeds then grow into new plants. If you look closely at a flower, you will see all the parts it needs for making seeds.

Parts of a flower

1 Stamens grow from the middle of the flower. Yellow powder called pollen is made on the tip of the stamens. Pollen gives some people hayfever.

Pollen

Stamen

2 Petals use colors, smells, and patterns to attract insects and birds that feed on pollen and on a sweet juice made by the plant, called nectar.

Ovary

Stem

Petal

Stamen

3 A stigma also grows from the middle of the flower. Pollen grains that land on the stigma grow a tube down to join an egg in the ovary. The egg can then become a seed.

4 The ovary is the case where eggs that become seeds are made.

From stigma

Ovary

Pollen fertilizes an egg to make a seed.

Flower power

Look for flowers of all colors, shapes, sizes, and smells growing in different places in the yard.

Apple blossom

Apple blossoms on an apple tree become fruit in the summer.

Daffodil bulbs can be planted in pots and window boxes.

Daffodil

Honeysuckle grows up walls and fences. It smells very sweet.

Honeysuckle

Stigma

Feeding birds

Birds are visitors to the yard, looking for food and water. In the spring, they may find a sheltered place there to build a nest. You can make sure there is always something for birds to eat and drink.

Winter bird cake

1 In winter, there is less food for birds to find. Use breadcrumbs from a stale loaf, uncooked peanuts, bacon rind, and fat to make a winter bird cake.

2 Line a cake pan or muffin tray with wax paper. Now mix the breadcrumbs, peanuts, and chopped bacon rind together in a bowl.

3 Fat will hold the cake together as well as keep the birds warm when they eat it. Melt the fat in a saucepan over a low heat until it is all liquid.

5 Let the mixture cool. Then turn it out of the tray and put your winter cake outside, out of reach of cats. Put out water, too.

4 Stir the melted fat into the dry mixture and pour it into the cake pan or muffin tray.

Bird food

Birds will find things to eat all over the yard.

Some birds feed on berries and fruit. Some catch insects in the air.

Caterpillars, snails, and worms make a juicy meal.

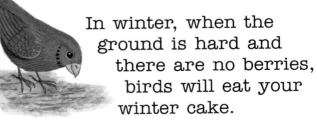

Small birds peck for seeds and insects on the ground.

In winter, when the ground is hard and there are no berries, birds will eat your winter cake.

Footprints

Birds are not the only visitors to the backyard who come looking for food and water. Other shy creatures come at night or when there is no one around. Their footprints will let you know who visited.

Hungry visitors

1 Fill a baking tray with damp sand and smooth it over. Put food scraps like brown bread, fruit, vegetables, and nuts on a plate. Pour milk or water into a saucer.

2 Put the food and liquid onto the baking tray and leave it in a quiet part of the yard. Check the tray for footprints in the morning and again in the evening.

3 Make a note of who has left tracks in the sand. Did they come at night or during the day? Look carefully, then smooth over the sand.

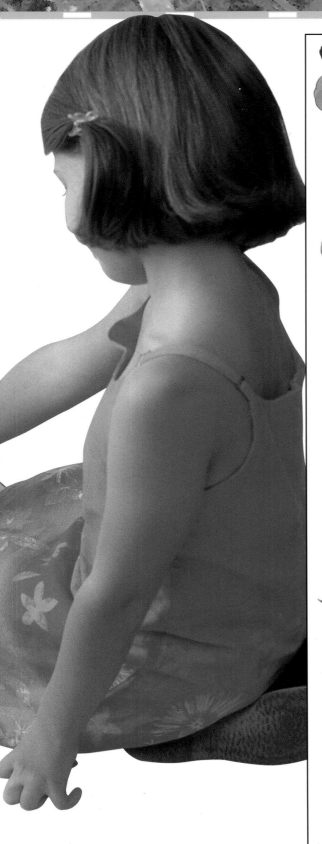

Identifying tracks

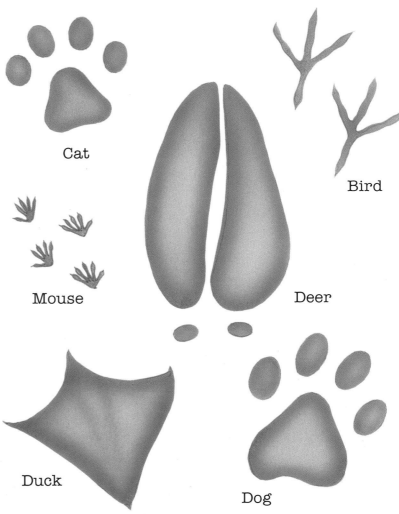

You can use these pictures to identify the footprints that have been made in your tray. These pictures are the same size as real animal footprints.

Cat

Bird

Mouse

Deer

Duck

Dog

If you can't see a print to match the ones in your tray, try to find the one that looks most like it. Can you tell if it is a bird or an animal? Is it big or small? Ask an adult to help you work out what any mystery prints are. You could look them up in a field guide.

Insect visitors

Look for insects in the soil, under stones, on plants, resting on walls, hiding in cracks, or swimming in water. Make a chart of the insects that live in or visit the backyard.

Spot the insects

Where insects live

			Dragonfly	Moth
(leaf)				x
(grass)		) x		
(flower)				
(brick wall)				
(pond)	x			

1 You will need a sheet of cardboard, a ruler, colored markers, and a magnifying glass.

2 Copy the chart in the picture onto your cardboard. You can add extra columns. Draw a moon if you spot an insect like a moth at night.

3 Look for insects in the backyard. Mark a cross on the chart to show what they are feeding on. What part of the yard has the most visitors? Do the insects come during the day or at night?

	Ladybug	Wasp	Butterfly
			x
		x	

A bug's parts

Insects all have six legs. They have a skeleton on the outside of their bodies and sensitive feelers called antennae. Many have wings.

Wasp

Thorax — Wing — Abdomen — Leg

Antenna — Compound eye

Insects can look very different from each other. Beetles have hard, shiny cases to protect their delicate wings. The easiest way to tell if a creature is an insect is to count its legs.

Beetle

Minibeasts

There are many small creatures, such as spiders and slugs, that are not insects. Spiders spin silky webs to catch their food. Slugs and snails slither along on silvery trails. Millipedes scuttle in dark, damp places. Set a trap to catch some minibeasts in your backyard.

Setting a trap

1 Dig a hole in the soil just deep enough to hold a small container. Put in pieces of fruit and a spoonful of cat food or dog food.

2 Cover the trap with a small rock, propping up one end with a stone to leave a small gap.

3 Leave the trap overnight. Lift the rock to see what you have caught. Before you let your minibeasts go, try to find out what they are.

Minibeast spotting

Use a magnifying glass and see if you can spot some of these creatures in your backyard.

A snail hides inside its shell when it is in danger.

Snail

Spiders are not insects because they have eight legs.

Spider

Millipedes, with hundreds of legs, eat leaves and dead plants.

Millipede

Slugs come out to look for food after rain.

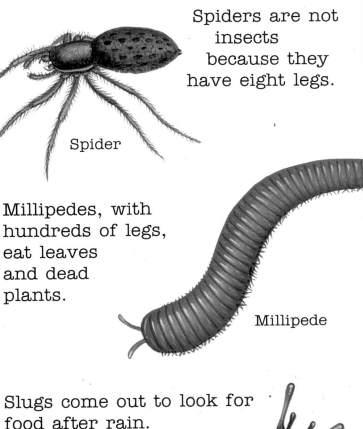

Slug

Ants

Ants have six legs, so you know they are insects. Ants often move around in long trails, following the same path. This project will help you find out if there is a busy ants' nest in your backyard.

Bait

Bait

Nest

Bait

Ant trails

1 Mix two teaspoons of sugar in a bowl half filled with warm water. Stir until the sugar dissolves.

2 Add small pieces of stale bread and leave them to soak for a few moments. Remove the bread before it gets too soggy and take it into the yard.

3 Put pieces of bread all over the yard as bait. Ants will find the food and carry it off, moving in a line. If you follow the line, you will find the ants' nest.

4 Draw a map of where you put the bread bait. Put in lines to show the paths the ants took to carry their food. The nest should be where all the lines meet.

Bait

Bait

Ants' nests

Ants live and work together in a nest underground. They build lots of tunnels. A queen ant lays eggs. Worker ants look for food and bring it back home along the tunnels.

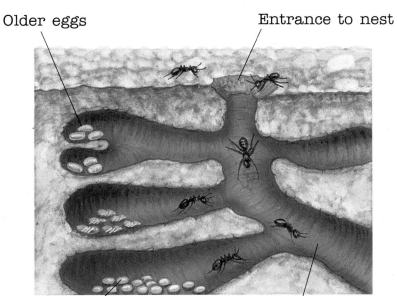

Older eggs

Entrance to nest

Young eggs

Main tunnel

Worms

As worms burrow along under the ground, they eat soil, leaving behind mounds of fine soil called worm casts. You can watch worms pull leaves and dead plants down into the soil to munch.

Worm watching

1 You will need a shoe box, a plastic trash bag, plastic wrap, leaves, tape, dead plants, soil, and worms.

2 Line the box with the plastic trash bag and secure it in place with tape. This will make the box waterproof.

3 Fill the box with damp soil and put in some worms you have dug up from the soil in the yard.

4 Let the worms burrow down into the soil, then sprinkle on the plants and leaves.

5 Cover the box with plastic wrap punched with holes to let in air. How long does it take for the leaves and plants to disappear?

Words on worms

Worms are not garden pests. Gardeners are very happy to have worms in the soil because they help to break it up. Breaking up the soil keeps it full of air, which is good for growing plants. Soil without any worms in it is solid, very heavy to dig, and not as good for growing things.

Chapter 4:
LIFE CYCLES

Animals and plants are alive, so we call them living things. All living things go through a life cycle. You can have fun learning about the different stages that animals and plants go through during their life cycles. You can also see what they need to grow and develop.

Contents

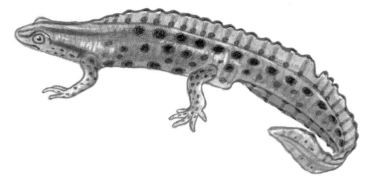

WHEEL OF LIFE 84

Make a life-cycle wheel.

REPRODUCTION 86

Look at who produces eggs.

GROWING UP 88

Make your own life scrapbook.

FOOD FOR GROWTH 90

Find out why we eat the food we do.

PLANTS AND SEEDS 92

Grow your own beans.

GROWING PLANTS 94

Find out what plants need to grow.

GROWING WITHOUT SEEDS 96

Make a potato maze.

BIRD NESTS 98

See what birds use to build nests.

NEWTS AND SNAKES 100

Learn about amphibians and reptiles.

BUTTERFLIES 102

Look at a butterfly's life cycle.

FOOD WEB 104

Build your own food web.

Wheel of life

Life cycles are made up of the stages that all living things go through as they grow and develop. Build a wheel of life to show how a living thing starts its life, then grows into an adult that can start another new life.

Life-cycle wheel

1 You will need two pieces of colored cardboard. Draw around a plate to make two circles and cut them out.

Get an adult to help you

2 Use a ruler to draw lines from top to bottom and side to side of one of the circles. This divides it into quarters. On the other circle, cut out a window. Decorate the rest of the circle.

3 In each quarter, draw a picture of one stage of the life cycle of a living thing. This wheel shows the life cycle of a flower called a pansy.

•A bee lands on a pansy.

•The bee carries pollen to another pansy.

•The pansy makes seeds, dies, and the seeds fall to the ground.

•A new pansy plant shoots up.

4 Join the circles at the center with a paper fastener. Turn the top circle clockwise to watch your wheel go around. Make more wheels to show other life cycles.

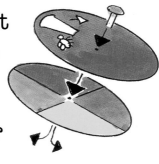

Pollen and seeds

A flower like a pansy makes new seeds when a bee rubs pollen from another pansy onto it.

Stigma

Ovary

The pollen rubs off the bee onto a part of the flower called the stigma. From there, it moves down inside the flower to the ovary, where the new seeds are made.

Pollen

Reproduction

For life to go on, living things must reproduce. This means they must make a new baby or plant like themselves. New life usually begins in an egg inside a mother's body. The egg can start to grow when a seed from a male joins it.

WASH YOUR HANDS AFTER TOUCHING RAW EGG

Inside a hen's egg

1 Crack open a hen's egg onto a white plate. Try not to break the yolk. The shell protects the delicate inside.

A red spot inside the yolk is the growing baby chick, called an embryo.

Eggs

Many animals lay eggs. Some time later, the eggs hatch. Other baby creatures grow inside their mothers' bodies.

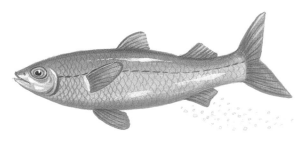

Fish lay a great number of eggs. The eggs float in the water and many are eaten by hungry sea creatures.

Female insects lay tiny eggs and leave them to hatch on their own.

Birds build nests to lay their eggs in. The mother and father birds often take turns to keep the eggs warm and safe.

People and many other animals don't lay eggs. Instead, the egg is inside the mother. When seed, called sperm, from the father joins the egg, a new baby starts to grow. It grows inside the mother until it is ready to be born.

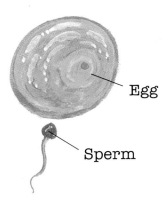

Egg

Sperm

The yellow yolk is food for the embryo.

The egg white is like a cushion around the embryo.

2 Look at the inside of the egg. The egg is full of food for the growing chick. Now cook and eat the egg.

Growing up

It takes many years for a human baby to become an adult. You have grown and changed a great deal since the day you were born. You will stop growing one day but you will never stop changing and learning.

Life scrapbook

1 Stick a picture of you as a baby into a scrapbook. Write down how much you weighed.

2 Ask a friend to draw around your feet on paper. Cut out the shapes and stick them into your scrapbook.

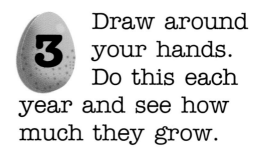

3 Draw around your hands. Do this each year and see how much they grow.

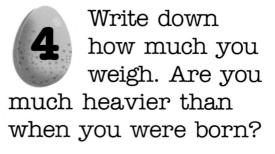

4 Write down how much you weigh. Are you much heavier than when you were born?

Big and small

All animals grow from babies to adults. Some grow much faster than others.

Elephants

An elephant can live for 75 years. A baby stays with its mother for up to ten years.

Mice

After only three weeks, baby mice have to leave their nest to look for their own food.

Parrots

Parrots can live for a very long time. Some have lived to be 80 years old.

Mayflies

Mayflies are born, live their life, and die all in one day. They have one of the shortest lifetimes of any creature.

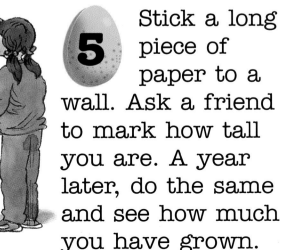

5 Stick a long piece of paper to a wall. Ask a friend to mark how tall you are. A year later, do the same and see how much you have grown.

Food for growth

You need to eat food from four food groups every day. Proteins help you grow and keep you healthy. Fats keep you warm. Carbohydrates give you energy and keep you going. Fruit and vegetables are full of vitamins.

Lunch boxes

1 Make sure that you pack your lunch box with a healthy meal. Cheese and ham in your sandwiches will give you protein and some fat. Bread will give you carbohydrate.

2 Cheese, yogurt, and butter are all made from milk. They give you protein and some fat. You should also drink plenty of water every day.

Carnivores and herbivores

Animals eat different kinds of food. Animals that eat meat are called carnivores. Animals that just eat plants are called herbivores.

A tiger is a carnivore. It hunts and kills its prey for food.

Sheep are herbivores. They graze on grass.

3 Fruit and vegetables give you vitamins, minerals, and roughage. Roughage helps your food pass easily through your body.

Ladybugs are carnivores. They feed on tiny bugs called aphids. Aphids suck juice called sap from plants.

4 A lot of salt and sugar is not good for you, so don't pack too many cookies and salty snacks.

A giraffe is a herbivore. It stretches its long neck to reach up to eat leaves from tall trees.

Plants and seeds

A bean is a kind of seed that you find inside a bean pod. Plant a bean from a pack and watch it grow into a new bean plant. Look carefully at the different stages the bean goes through.

Plant a bean

1 You will need cotton balls, a glass jar, and beans from a pack.

2 Soak the beans in water overnight to soften their tough skin. Line the jar with cotton. Pour in water until the cotton is damp but not soaking wet.

3 Space the beans around the edge of the jar. Put the jar on a windowsill. Dampen the cotton every day.

4 After a few days, the beans will begin to sprout. Make a diary of how they grow. Watch how the roots grow down before the shoots begin to grow up.

Life cycle of a flowering plant

The life cycle of a nasturtium flower follows the same pattern as many other flowering plants.

Spring is the time for seeds under the earth to start growing.

 A shoot pushes through the earth toward the light.

In warm weather, flowers bloom. Insects feed on a sweet juice made by the flower, called nectar.

 Frost kills the plant, and its seeds fall to the earth where they rest until spring.

Growing plants

Plants need sunlight, water, air, and nutrients from the soil to be able to make their own food and grow. Without even one of these, the plant will not be strong and healthy and may even die. Find out what happens to a plant without sunlight, water, or air.

Happy plants

1 You will need four young plants. Water the first one. Leave it in an airy place in sunlight. Watch how well it grows.

2 Put the second plant next to the first, but don't water it. It will soon start to wilt.

3 Water the third plant, but put a box over it. The green will fade and the plant will begin to die.

Plant survival

Plants have found ways of surviving in all corners of the earth.

Desert plants have long roots. These search for water, which is stored in fleshy stems.

Rain-forest creepers with shiny leaves climb up the tall trees toward the sunlight.

Mountain plants grow close to the ground or in cracks away from cold winds.

4 Spread petroleum jelly on a leaf of the last plant so that air can't get to it. Watch the leaf shrivel after a few days.

Growing without seeds

Some plants can grow new plants without seeds. A potato is a root that is packed with the food that the new potato plant needs in order to grow. It has little buds called eyes.

A potato maze

1 You can grow a new potato plant from an old potato. You will need a potato with eyes, a shoe box with a lid, cardboard, scissors, and tape.

Get an adult to help you

2 Cut three strips of cardboard for the maze and make a hole in one end of the box.

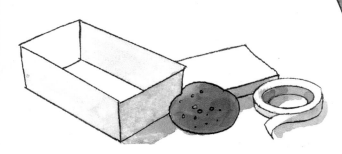

3 Bend the end of each strip of cardboard to make a flap. Tape the flaps to the sides of the box.

4 Place the potato in the box and put on the lid. After a few days, shoots will start to grow from the eyes up through the maze toward the light.

Light

New plants from old plants

New plants can start to grow from parts of old plants.

A new garlic plant will grow from a piece of a garlic bulb.

You can grow a new African violet plant from a leaf planted in soil.

Strawberry plants grow long stems called runners. New little plants grow along the runners.

A piece of a geranium plant will grow roots if you put it in water or plant it.

Shoots will grow from a carrot top if you put it in water.

Bird nests

All birds lay eggs. Most birds build a nest to keep their eggs safe and warm until they hatch. Put out some materials in spring and see which ones a bird will choose to build its nest.

Bird box

1 Ask an adult to make or buy a strong bird box. Mount it securely on a tree where it is safe from cats.

2 Collect materials like straw, cotton balls, dry leaves, hay, feathers, yarn, shredded paper, or even hair from a hairbrush.

3 Spread your materials on the ground around the nesting box. See which ones the birds choose. Birds mostly use natural materials like sticks, leaves, mud, and moss to build their nests.

4 Watch the birds carry the materials into the nesting box. Some may take the nesting materials to build a nest nearby.

Life cycle of a blue tit

Like all birds, a blue tit begins its life inside an egg.

The adult bird keeps the egg warm until it hatches.

The egg hatches into a hungry baby bird called a nestling.

The young bird begins to look for its own food and learns to fly. It is now a fledgling.

It can soon manage without help from its mother and father.

The adult bird finds a mate. The female lays eggs in the spring.

Newts and snakes

Newts, frogs, and toads all belong to a group of animals called amphibians. They lay their eggs, called spawn, in water. Baby amphibians live underwater. As adults, they live in water and on land. Reptiles, like snakes, have scaly skins and lay eggs.

Life cycle of a newt

1 A female newt lays hundreds of eggs on underwater plants. The eggs are surrounded by jelly.

2 Baby newts begin to grow inside the eggs. They feed on the jelly until they hatch out as tadpoles.

3 Newt tadpoles have gills to let them breathe underwater, like fish. They grow lungs to let them breathe air, and they also grow legs.

4 Adult newts live on land. They go back into the water only to keep their skin wet and to lay eggs.

Life cycle of a snake

1 Snakes are reptiles. They lay their eggs on the ground and then leave the eggs to hatch by themselves.

2 Newly hatched snakes are called hatchlings. They look just like tiny adult snakes.

4 Snakes grow and shed their skin all their lives. Adult snakes lay eggs, and a new life cycle begins.

3 As snakes grow, they shed their skin. They grow a new skin, wriggle out of the old skin, and leave it behind in one piece.

Other reptile eggs

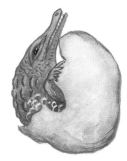

Crocodiles lay their eggs in sand. When they hatch, the mother carries them in her mouth to the water.

Mother turtles bury their eggs in the sand, then swim away. The hatchlings make their own way down to the sea.

Butterflies

Some creatures change shape as they become adults. Tadpoles become frogs, and caterpillars become butterflies. This change of shape is called metamorphosis. Find a caterpillar eating leaves. You may be able to follow its metamorphosis into a butterfly.

2 Caterpillars hatch and feed on the leaves where the eggs were laid.

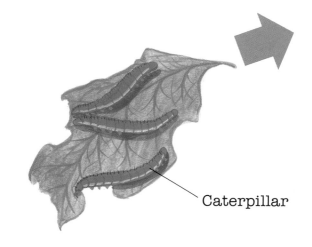

Caterpillar

Life cycle of a butterfly

1 The male butterfly finds a female butterfly to mate with. After mating, the female lays her eggs on a leaf, then flies off.

Eggs

3 Each caterpillar hangs by a silk thread and turns into a chrysalis. Inside the chrysalis, amazing changes take place.

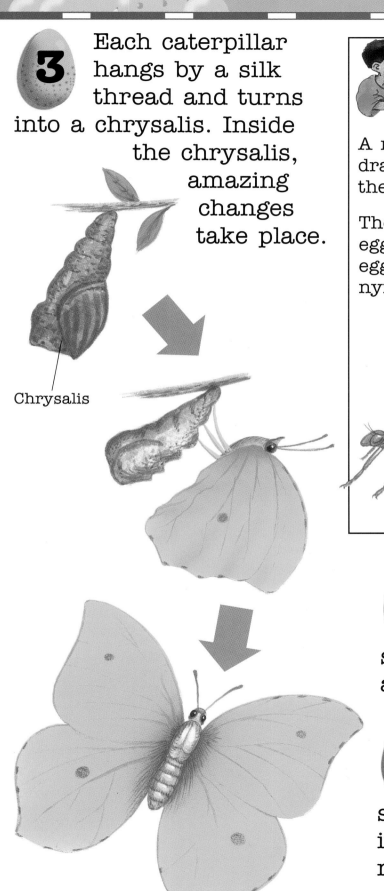

Chrysalis

Dragonfly

A dragonfly is another insect that changes shape.

A male and a female dragonfly mate as they fly through the air.

The female lays her eggs underwater. The eggs hatch into nymphs.

A nymph spends a year underwater. It climbs a reed, splits its skin, and comes out as a dragonfly.

4 A butterfly struggles out of the chrysalis, dries its wings in the sun, and flies away.

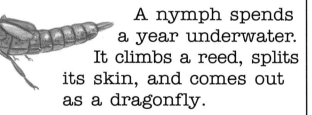

5 Butterflies often live for only a short time. They have an important job to do. They must start a new life cycle.

Food web

All living things depend on the sun. Plants use the sun's energy to make their food. Herbivores eat plants, and carnivores eat the plant eaters. Make a food web to see how life on earth is linked together.

Weave a web

1 Think of animals that live near each other to put in your food web. Draw or cut out pictures of them from magazines.

2 Draw and cut out pictures of air, water, the sun, and some plants. Glue all of your pictures onto folded strips of cardboard.

Get an adult to help you

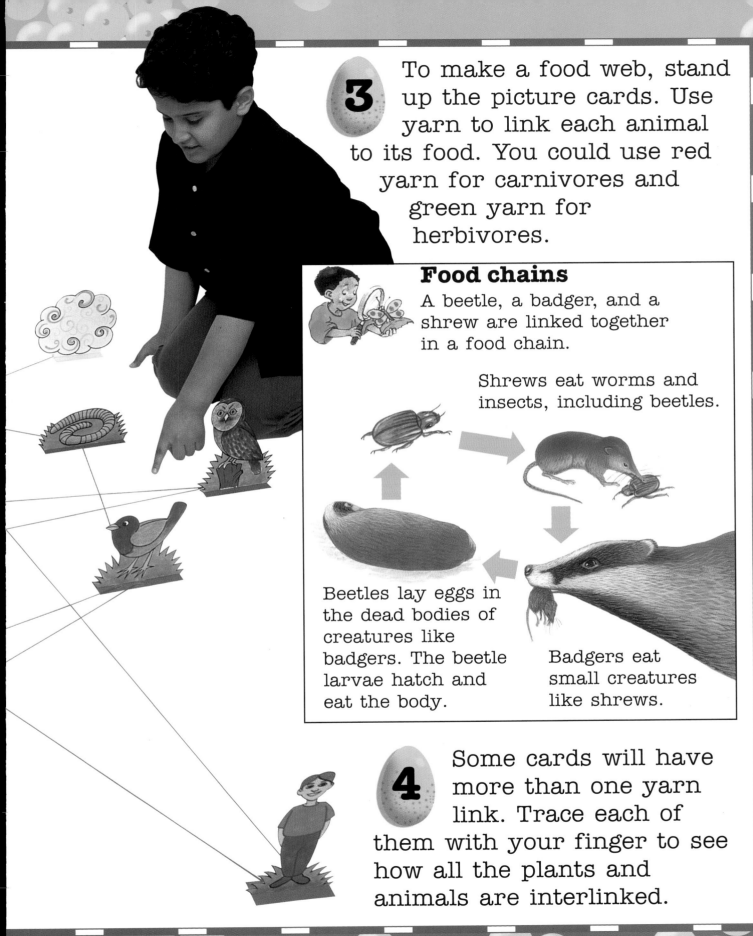

3 To make a food web, stand up the picture cards. Use yarn to link each animal to its food. You could use red yarn for carnivores and green yarn for herbivores.

Food chains

A beetle, a badger, and a shrew are linked together in a food chain.

Shrews eat worms and insects, including beetles.

Beetles lay eggs in the dead bodies of creatures like badgers. The beetle larvae hatch and eat the body.

Badgers eat small creatures like shrews.

4 Some cards will have more than one yarn link. Trace each of them with your finger to see how all the plants and animals are interlinked.

Chapter 5:
WOODS AND MEADOWS

Woods and meadows are places you can visit that are full of many different kinds of wildlife. You can have fun playing a guessing game about where animals live. Learn how to draw meadow flowers and how to look closely at tiny insects. See how to plant a tree and learn how to paint and cut out a camouflaged bird.

Contents

LIFE IN A TREE 108

Look at what lives in a tree.

DIFFERENT WOODLANDS 110

Make rubbings of different leaves.

THE WOODLAND FLOOR 112

See what you can find under a tree.

WOODLAND ANIMALS 114

Look for signs of woodland animals.

WOODLAND BIRDS 116

Learn about cuckoos and other birds.

PLANT A TREE 118

Collect and plant tree seeds.

GRASSES 120

Make a grasses guessing game.

MEADOW FLOWERS 122

Learn about some meadow flowers.

MEADOW INSECTS 124

Sweep meadow grasses for insects.

MEADOW BIRDS 126

Paint a camouflaged bird.

MEADOW ANIMALS 128

Make a meadow mix and match.

Life in a tree

Trees are the biggest plants on the earth. They can live to be very old. All kinds of plants and animals live in the different parts of a tree. Find out which creatures have made their home in a tree near you.

Shake a limb

1 You need a magnifying glass and a large sheet of cardboard. Lay the cardboard under a low branch of a tree.

2 Shake the branch gently. Look through the magnifying glass at the creatures that fall onto the cardboard. Try to find out what each one is.

Tree creatures

Small creatures can find food in every part of a tree. Sometimes, too many insects can kill a tree.

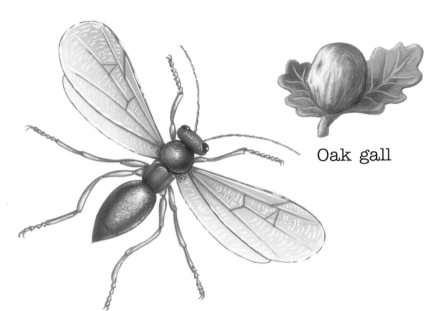

Oak gall

Adult bark beetles feed on buds and new leaves. Their tiny young, called larvae, live in the tree trunk and chew wood.

Gall wasp grubs live inside oak galls. They come out when they have grown into adult gall wasps.

A nut weevil drills a tiny hole and lays its eggs inside a nut such as an acorn. The grubs use the nut for food.

Caterpillars that are the same color as leaves or twigs can be difficult to spot. Holes in the leaves tell you where they have been feeding.

Hole

Acorn

3 Now look up into the branches, in the bark, and around the roots. What other creatures can you see?

PUT CREATURES BACK WHERE YOU FOUND THEM

Different woodlands

Trees grow together to form different kinds of woodland. You can tell what kind of woodland you are in by the shape of the leaves. Deciduous trees have wide, flat leaves. Evergreen trees often have tough, shiny leaves.

Sorting and rubbing leaves

1 Try to visit different kinds of woodland. Pick up leaves from the woodland floor.

2 Sort your leaves into piles of different shapes. Use a book to find out which trees they come from. Are they from deciduous or evergreen trees?

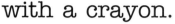 **3** Make leaf rubbings by laying paper over each leaf, with the rough side of the leaf facing upward. Rub evenly over the paper with a crayon.

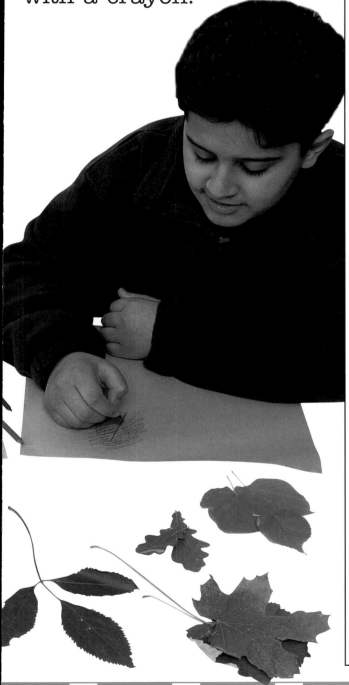

Deciduous and evergreen trees

The leaves on deciduous trees change color in the fall, then fall off the tree in winter. Evergreen trees keep their leaves all year round. Conifers, such as pine trees, are evergreens. They have long, thin leaves called needles.

Sugar maple   Horse chestnut

Sugar maples and horse chestnuts are deciduous trees.

Scots pine   Holly

Scots pines and holly trees are evergreens. Even evergreen trees will shed a few leaves as new ones grow.

The woodland floor

In early spring, before leaves have grown on the trees, the floor in deciduous woods is filled with light. Evergreen woods are always quite dark as the leaves keep out the light. See what you can find on different woodland floors.

Circle a tree

1 To see what lies under a tree, you can circle it. You will need thick string, twigs, a notebook, and a pencil.

2 Press the twigs firmly into the ground around a tree. Loop the string on the ground around the twigs to make a circle.

3 Look carefully at the ground inside the string circle. Draw or make a note of what you see.

Mosses, lichens, and ferns

Mosses, lichens, and ferns are all plants that have no flowers. Look out for them growing on a woodland floor.

Lichens grow on rocks, trees, and soil. They grow very slowly and live for a long time.

Mosses spread over damp ground and on wet logs.

Ferns can grow in many different kinds of soil. Their tightly curled stems open out into green fronds.

DON'T TOUCH DROPPINGS OR FUNGI

4 Use your notes to make a chart of the area under the tree. Draw a circle on a piece of cardboard for the string. Fill in all the things you saw.

Woodland animals

Woodland animals are usually very shy. There are plenty of places to hide in the woods, so they are hard to spot. But you can listen and look for signs that tell you they are not far away.

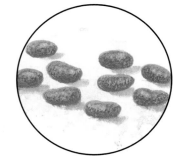

Deer droppings

Spot the signs

1 Look for deer droppings and footprints. A tree with no low-growing leaves might have been browsed (eaten) by a passing deer. In some places, you can spot where a deer has nibbled a ring of bark from a young tree. This can sometimes kill the tree.

Deer browse low-growing leaves into a straight line.

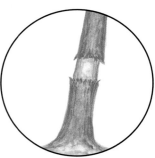

Bark nibbled by deer

2 Badgers look for food at night. They live in holes called sets. See if you can spot bits of plants that they drag into their sets for bedding. Look for badger fur caught on wire.

Squirrel food litter

Squirrel drey

3 Squirrels dart along branches and up and down tree trunks. They build homes called dreys high up in trees. Look under trees for nuts and cones they have dropped.

DO NOT TOUCH BARBED WIRE

Hunters and hunted

Foxes and wolves hunt and kill animals that feed on woodland plants. People hunt and eat woodland deer and wild boar.

A red fox has pointed ears and sharp eyes to listen and look for prey.

A boar is a kind of wild pig. It uses its blunt snout to root for food on the woodland floor.

A wood mouse has sharp teeth for nibbling seeds and nuts. It has to watch out for hungry foxes.

Woodland birds

Woods are good places to look for birds. Walk quietly because sudden noises and movements will frighten them away. In spring, birds build nests in hollow trunks or branches. In summer and fall, they find insects, seeds, nuts, and berries to eat. In winter, they find shelter in the trees.

Cuckoo

1 Cuckoos fly south in winter to find food in warmer places. In spring, they fly back north to breed.

2 The mother cuckoo looks for a nest belonging to another bird. She throws out an egg from the nest, lays one of her own in its place, then flies off.

Sights and sounds

Sometimes it is hard to spot birds through the leaves, especially in darker evergreen woods. Look for flashes of color as they fly past, and listen for the noises they make.

A woodpigeon makes a soft cooing sound. It hops and flies up in the branches, but finds its food on the ground.

Jays are colorful crows and have a harsh cry. They will eat eggs from the nests of smaller birds.

You can hear woodpeckers tapping at tree trunks as they look for insects or drill out a nest hole.

Crossbills live in coniferous forests. They use their crossed bills to pick out the seeds from cones.

3 The cuckoo chick hatches and grows quickly. It pushes the other eggs and smaller chicks out of the nest.

4 The adopted parent birds are kept very busy feeding their big, hungry cuckoo chick.

Plant a tree

In the fall, look for acorns, horse chestnuts, and sycamore "wings" on the woodland floor. They are all different seeds that will grow into new young trees in the spring. Collect some seeds and try to grow trees from them.

See it grow

1 In the spring, push your seeds into the soil, about 1 inch deep. Trees grow very tall, so leave enough room around each one for roots and branches to spread.

2 Make labels and push them into the soil next to the seeds. An acorn grows into an oak tree and a horse chestnut into a horse chestnut tree.

SCOTS PINE

HORSE CHESTNUT

CHESTNUT

OAK

3 Trees grow slowly, so be patient. Some seeds may not grow at all. Make a chart to record the growth of your first shoot.

Tree rings

Each year, a new layer grows around a tree trunk and makes a ring. By counting the rings inside the trunk of a fallen tree, you can tell the tree's age.

It would take a long time to count the rings of giant trees called sequoias – they can live for over a thousand years.

119

Grasses

The grass in your local park or yard is just one of more than ten thousand different kinds of grasses. Grazing animals like sheep, horses, and cows eat grass. But did you know that you eat grass, too?

Grasses we eat

1 Wheat, rice, corn, and oats are grasses that farmers grow for us to eat. Copy pictures of them onto four pieces of cardboard and label them.

Wheat | Corn | Rice | Oats

A   B   C   D

2 Pour some dry rice, popcorn kernels, flour (or wheat grains), and dry oatmeal in four piles on a piece of cardboard.

Answers:
A = rice
B = wheat grains
C = oats
D = corn kernels

3 Now ask a friend to match each of the four piles to the picture of the crop it came from.

From field to food

All over the world, farmers grow different kinds of grasses for food. These are called cereal crops. The ripe seeds are the grains. They give us some of our most important food.

Wheat is grown in enormous fields. The grains are ground into flour to make bread and pasta.

Rice is grown underwater in fields called paddies. We cook rice or grind the grains to make breakfast cereals.

Corn gives us corn on the cob, which is good to cook and eat. The grains can be ground into flour.

Oatmeal comes from oats. We use it to make hot cereal and cookies.

Meadow flowers

In the summer, you can see colorful flowers dotted among the tall meadow grasses. They are bright red, blue, purple, and yellow to attract insects. See how many different flowers of each color you can find in a summer meadow.

Flower sketching

1 To sketch flowers, you will need a sketchbook, some colored pencils, and an eraser. Before you start sketching, study the color of the flowers, how many petals each one has, and the shape of their leaves.

Dandelion

Flower

Leaf

Wild flowers

A gardener chooses which flowers to grow in a garden. Meadow flowers grow naturally by spreading their seeds.

The common milkweed grows wild in North America. Soft floss from its seedpods is used for stuffing furniture.

Meadow buttercups have shiny yellow petals. If you hold one under your chin, it makes your skin look yellow like butter.

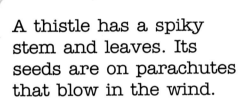

A thistle has a spiky stem and leaves. Its seeds are on parachutes that blow in the wind.

Look closely at a scabious flower to see that it is made up of a mass of tiny flowers.

Poppy

Flower

Seed head

2 Copy the flowers as carefully and accurately as you can. You can look up any of the ones you don't know in a flower book later.

DO NOT PICK THE FLOWERS

Meadow insects

There are insects all over a meadow. Butterflies fly among the flowers, beetles scuttle along the ground, and bugs crawl up stems. Insects too small to spot can be swept up in a net.

Insect sweep

1 To look closely at insects, you will need a net with a long handle, a large sheet of paper, and a magnifying glass.

BE CAREFUL OF INSECTS THAT STING

Froghopper

Horsefly

Lacewing

2 Sweep the net with a long stroke across the top of meadow grasses. Tip out what you have caught onto the paper.

Brimstone butterfly

Hoverflies

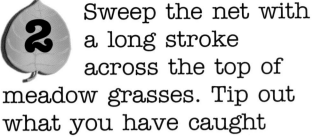

Grasshoppers

If you listen carefully, you are sure to hear grasshoppers chirping in a summer meadow. Grasshoppers call to each other either by rubbing their wings together or by rubbing part of their back legs against their wings. They have long, very strong back legs for hopping through the grass.

Grasshopper

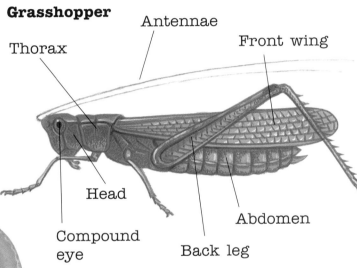

Thorax
Antennae
Front wing
Head
Compound eye
Back leg
Abdomen

A type of grasshopper called a locust is a pest to farmers in many places. Locusts travel in vast swarms and can eat and destroy whole fields of crops.

3 Look carefully at the insects with your magnifying glass. When you have finished, tip them gently back onto the grass.

Meadow birds

Some birds visit meadows to eat seeds, worms, snails, and insects. Other birds build their nests there. The color of their feathers helps them to hide in the grass. This is called camouflage.

Camouflage a bird

1 You will need four big sheets of cardboard, paints, and scissors. Paint tall grasses onto one sheet of cardboard.

2 When the paint is dry, draw on a bird shape. Cut it out to leave a bird-shaped hole.

3 Paint the other three pieces of cardboard with different coloured splotches, as shown in the main picture. Use clean water for each color.

Birds in the grass

You can watch flocks of birds fly in and feed together in meadows all year round.

Canada geese arrive in flocks and graze on the grass. They make a loud, honking noise.

A skylark disguises where its nest is on the ground by landing away from it and then running to it through the grass.

Crows nest in platforms of sticks in treetops. They feed together in meadows, eating insects and seeds.

Lapwings sometimes arrive to feed in flocks of thousands. They are sometimes called "peewits" because of the sound they make.

4 Put each colored cardboard behind the cardboard with the bird cut out of it. Some colors will camouflage the bird in the grass better than others.

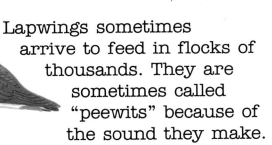

Meadow animals

Grass snakes, moles, rabbits, and foxes are all animals you might see in a meadow. They live in holes underground. Animal droppings or fur around a hole may let you know who lives there.

Match the homes

1 Draw pictures of a grass snake, a mole, a rabbit, and a fox on four pieces of cardboard. Cut them out.

2 Each animal digs a different shaped tunnel or hole. Copy a grass snake nest, a mole nest, a rabbit warren, and a fox lair onto four other pieces of cardboard.

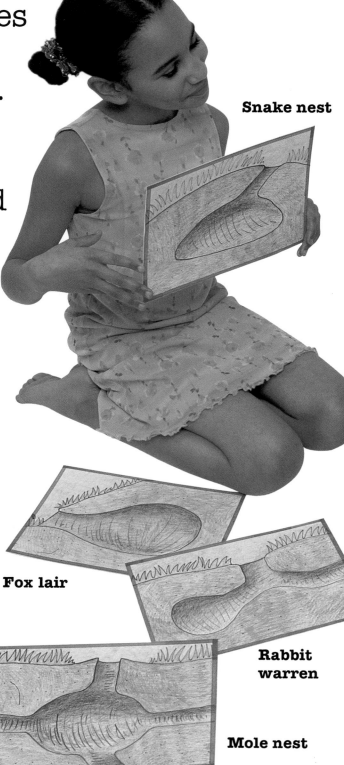

Snake nest

Fox lair

Rabbit warren

Mole nest

The harvest mouse

The tiny harvest mouse lives among the grass stalks in fields or meadows.

It hangs onto the stalks with its tail and back legs and uses its front paws to eat the grains.

The mother harvest mouse weaves a round nest made of grass or reed stalks for her babies. In places with hedgerows, she may build a more secure nest by winding stalks of grass around the thicker stalks in the hedge.

3 Hold up each of your tunnel pictures in turn. Ask a friend to match each animal to its home.

Get an adult to help you

Chapter 6: ALL YEAR ROUND

As the seasons change, you can see differences in the plants and animals around you. Have fun keeping a nature diary, and build a museum of the seasons. Paint summer sunflower pots, make pictures from leaves in the fall, and see how you can help animals keep warm in winter. Listen to the changing noises through the year, and learn about migration.

Contents

NATURE DIARY **132**

Make a picture diary each month.

WINDOW BOX **134**

Plant an herb window box.

SEASONAL SOUNDS **136**

Listen to the sounds of nature.

SUNFLOWERS **138**

Paint pots and grow sunflowers.

NECTAR EATERS **140**

Which creatures eat nectar?

COLLECTIONS **142**

Make a museum of the seasons.

FRUIT SALAD **144**

Collect seeded fruits and make a fruit salad.

CHANGING COLOR **146**

Make lots of leaf pictures.

LOOKING FOR FOOD **148**

Learn about creatures that migrate.

HIBERNATION **150**

Build a shelter for a sleeping animal.

ASLEEP IN THE SOIL **152**

Grow a plant from a bulb.

Nature diary

Look and listen carefully and you will notice fascinating things happening in nature all year round. You can make a nature diary to keep a record of the things you spot at different times of year, both in the city and in the countryside.

Month by month

1 To make a nature diary, you will need a large pad, pen and pencils, glue, and tape. Make a page for each month like the one in the picture.

2 Collect leaves and pine needles from the ground. Leave them to dry, then glue them into your diary. Make sure you label them.

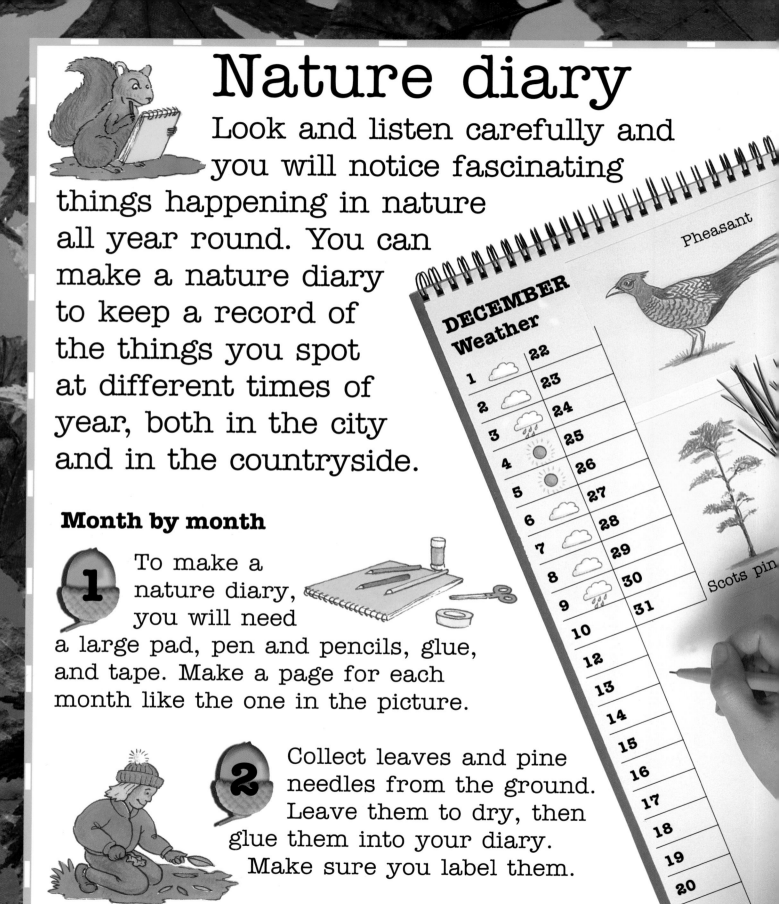

DECEMBER
Weather

Pheasant

Scots pine

Fern

Scots pine needles

Oak tree

NOTES:
2nd Dec: - Saw four pheasants pecking in a field.

Puddles frozen

Frost on the grass, bare trees

Keeping records

You can keep records for your nature diary in many different ways. The more ways you use, the more interesting your diary will be.

Hang a thermometer outside and record the temperature each day. Write down the different things you spot on hot and cold days.

Make sketches. You might not remember what you have seen after you get home. Glue the sketches into your diary.

If you have a camera, take photographs. You may notice something you didn't spot at first when you see the print.

3 Draw pictures and write notes about interesting things you see. Every day, copy one of the symbols below to show the weather.

Sunny   Cloudy   Rainy   Snowy   Stormy

Window box

You can grow plants all year round even if you don't have a backyard. Try planting herbs in a window box. When they have grown, pinch the leaves to smell the herbs' fragrance.

Indoors and outdoors

1 You will need packets of herb seeds and a window box with compost in it.

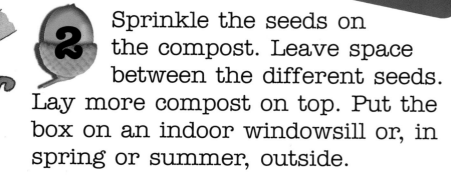

2 Sprinkle the seeds on the compost. Leave space between the different seeds. Lay more compost on top. Put the box on an indoor windowsill or, in spring or summer, outside.

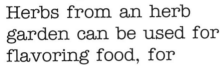 **4** When the herbs have grown, you can snip off the leaves to use for cooking. Only cut off what you need. The leaves will grow back again.

Herb garden

Herbs from an herb garden can be used for flavoring food, for brewing herbal teas, and for treating illnesses.

Rosemary tea is good for soothing headaches and upset stomachs.

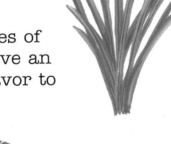

The leaves of chives give an onion flavor to salads.

3 Water the herbs regularly. If they are outside, check that there has been enough rain.

Parsley stalks have a stronger flavor than the leaves.

Basil is grown among other plants to keep insects away. You can add its leaves to tomato dishes.

Seasonal sounds

Go outside and listen carefully. Some sounds you hear are made by people or machines, but others are noises made by nature. Make a note of all the natural sounds you can hear at different times of the year.

Nightingale

Listen closely

1 In the early spring, listen for male birds singing to attract a mate. Later, baby birds cheep noisily for food.

Jay

2 In the summer, insects buzz among the flowers and grasshoppers sing in the grass.

Fly

Grasshopper

Geese

Croaking frogs

In the spring, male frogs gather together in ponds and croak loudly. Each one is trying to attract a female to mate with. They can even croak underwater.

Frog

Air sack

When a frog croaks, a pouch of skin under its chin fills with air and helps the croaking sound to carry over a distance. Some frogs are named after the sounds they make, such as the snoring puddle frog, which is found in parts of Africa.

3 In the fall, listen for wings beating as flocks of geese fly south for the winter. In woods, listen for nuts falling into crunchy leaves.

Chestnut

Rough ridges on the grasshopper's back legs rub against the wings to make a chirruping noise.

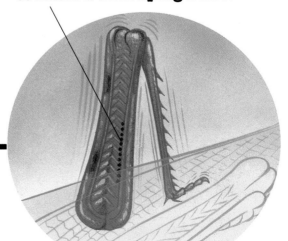

4 In winter, listen for the harsh caw of crows. They nest in the tops of trees and you can sometimes see them looking for food in trash.

Crow

Sunflowers

Sunflowers are very useful plants. Animals eat the leaves, yellow dye is made from the petals, and oil is pressed from the seeds. Plant a sunflower seed in spring, and by the summer it will have grown taller than you!

Painting and planting

1 You will need a packet of sunflower seeds, soil, three big flower pots, and paints.

2 Paint pictures of sunflowers on the outside of the pots. Plant two or three seeds in each pot. Water them regularly.

3 As the shoots appear, leave the strongest shoot in each pot to grow and pull up the others.

4 Your sunflowers will grow very tall. You can support the stems with sticks.

Follow the sun

Although sunflowers look like bright yellow suns, they are called sunflowers for another reason. In the morning, they face the rising sun. As the sun moves throughout the day, the sunflowers turn their heads to follow it across the sky.

Noon

Morning

Evening

5 After the petals die, leave the flower heads for the birds. They will eat the seeds that form in the middle of the sunflower.

Nectar eaters

Butterflies visit flowers in the daytime. Moths often feed at night. They use long feeding tubes like drinking straws to suck sweet juice called nectar from the flowers. Look for butterflies and moths when the flowers they feed on are in bloom.

Butterfly watching

1 Butterflies are attracted to purple flowers with a strong scent, like buddleia flowers. Buddleia is also called the butterfly bush.

2 Make sketches and take notes of butterflies you see. This will help you look them up later in a field guide.

3 Use binoculars to help you spot butterflies. This will let you see their markings more clearly and will let you watch without disturbing them. You might even see some having a drink from a puddle.

Feeding on flowers

Most butterflies live only for a short time in the summer when the flowers are out. Other creatures that drink nectar, such as hummingbirds, make long journeys to find flowers in bloom all year round.

Honeysuckle smells most strongly at night to attract moths.

Butterflies curl their feeding tubes under their heads when they are not in use.

Tiny Australian honey possums have long tongues to lick nectar from banksia flowers.

A hummingbird hovers in front of a flower while it sucks nectar with its long tongue.

Collections

Go for a walk at any time of year and you will find all kinds of interesting natural things. Make a collection for each season, or for places you visit like the park or the seashore.

Make a minimuseum

1 Find a cardboard box with a good sized base. Cut down the sides to make a frame.

2 Line the box with colored paper. This will be the background for your minimuseum.

Get an adult to help you

Cockleshell

Garden snail shell

Chestnut

Chestnut husk

Maple leaf

Cedar cone

142

3 Arrange the objects you have collected in the box. Then carefully glue them down. Label each item clearly.

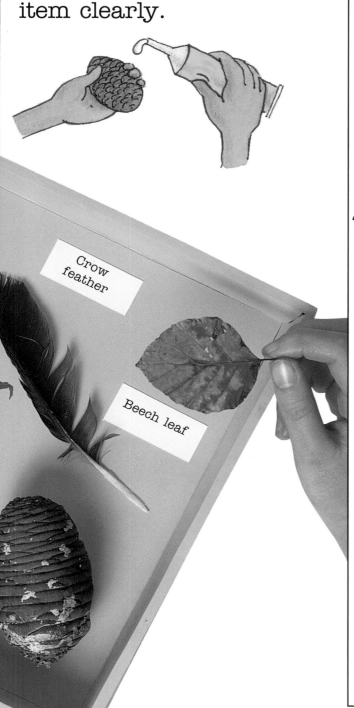

Crow feather

Beech leaf

Flying feathers

Birds are the only creatures that have feathers. Their feathers are shaped for the different jobs they have to do. You can tell which part of a bird's body a feather comes from.

Small covert feathers make the front of the wing smooth.

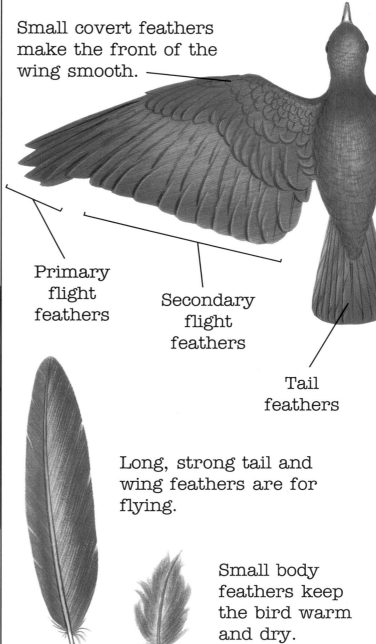

Primary flight feathers

Secondary flight feathers

Tail feathers

Long, strong tail and wing feathers are for flying.

Small body feathers keep the bird warm and dry.

Fruit salad

Fruit is the part of a plant that holds the seeds for a new plant to grow. When a flower dies, a fruit grows in its place. Tiny apples start to grow after the apple blossom dies in the spring. By fall, the apples are juicy and ready to eat.

Chop it up

1 Make a delicious fruit salad with lots of different fruits. First, cut each fruit in half or into quarters.

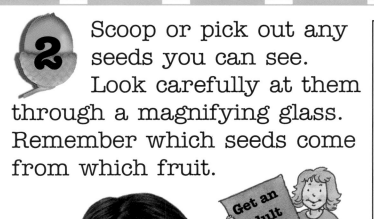

2 Scoop or pick out any seeds you can see. Look carefully at them through a magnifying glass. Remember which seeds come from which fruit.

Get an adult to help you

Wild berries

Wild berries are often bright and shiny. Birds spot them easily and swoop down to eat them. The birds then scatter plant seeds in their droppings, letting new plants grow.

In winter, bright red holly berries make a feast for hungry birds when there is little food around.

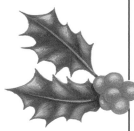

Mistletoe grows on the branches of other trees. Its white berries are poisonous to people and animals.

Blackberries grow wild on prickly brambles in early fall. Birds, animals, and people like to eat them.

SOME BERRIES ARE POISONOUS. ALWAYS ASK AN ADULT.

3 Ask a friend to match each seed to the fruit it came from.

Changing color

Trees make food using the green color in their leaves, called chlorophyll. In the summer, trees store the food they make. By the fall, the chlorophyll is not needed. It breaks down and turns the leaves red, brown, gold, and orange.

Leaf pictures

1 Collect as many different leaves in the fall as you can. Sort them into different shapes and colors.

2 You will need a clip frame and some colored paper. Cut out a piece of paper the same size as the clip frame and lay it over the base of the frame.

Winter leaves

By winter, most of the fallen leaves will have rotted away. Only leaf skeletons, evergreen leaves, and pine needles remain.

A leaf skeleton forms when the soft part of the leaf rots, leaving the tough stem and the veins.

Holly trees are evergreen. They keep their shiny, prickly leaves all year round.

Pine needles are very thin leaves that can survive the cold. They stay on the trees all winter.

3 Arrange the leaves into a pattern or a picture, then lay the glass on top. The glass will hold the leaves in position.

Get an adult to help you

Looking for food

In spring and summer, animals and birds can usually find plenty of food to eat. Many have to make long journeys to find enough food at other times of year. The journeys they make are called migrations.

Spot migrating birds

1 You can often identify different birds by the way they behave or fly. Before flying off, migrating swallows gather together on telephone wires.

Swallows

Geese

2 Migrating geese fly off together in a V shape. Watch for geese and swallows in the fall. Make picture cards to keep a record of all the migrating birds you spot.

Mexico

South America

Finding the way

Each year, animals, birds, and insects find their way across thousands of miles of land and sea. Whales swim halfway around the world and caribou travel between the Arctic plains and northern forests. Match the colored arrows to the arrows on the globe to see the migration routes.

Humpback whales follow the coastline on their journey between cold polar and warm tropical seas.

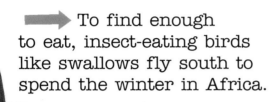

To find enough to eat, insect-eating birds like swallows fly south to spend the winter in Africa.

North Pole

Europe

Africa

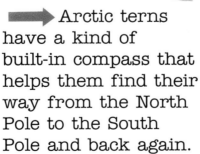

Arctic terns have a kind of built-in compass that helps them find their way from the North Pole to the South Pole and back again.

Caribou follow the same paths each year. They go south in the fall and back north again in the spring.

Monarch butterflies fly south from Canada in huge numbers, to spend the winter in Mexico.

Hibernation

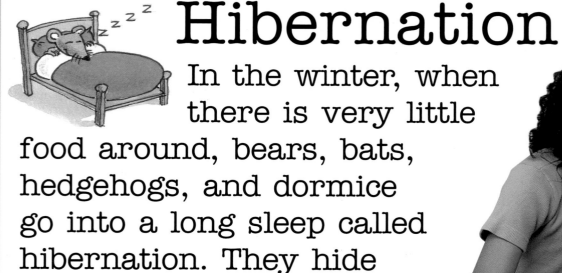

In the winter, when there is very little food around, bears, bats, hedgehogs, and dormice go into a long sleep called hibernation. They hide away in a safe, dry place and sleep until the warm spring weather wakes them up again.

The big sleep

1 Make an animal shelter in the fall. Collect dry sticks and some straw and leaves for warm bedding.

NEVER DISTURB A HIBERNATING ANIMAL

2 In a quiet place outside, make a strong frame with the sticks. Cover it with earth, grass, and leaves and put the bedding inside.

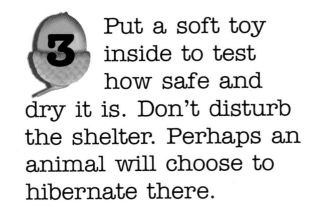

3 Put a soft toy inside to test how safe and dry it is. Don't disturb the shelter. Perhaps an animal will choose to hibernate there.

Winter and summer

Some animals hibernate together in winter. Some sleep in summer when water is scarce. This summer sleep is called estivation.

During the long winter sleep in her den, a mother bear wakes to give birth to her cubs.

During the winter, some kinds of bats hibernate together. They hang upside down in enormous groups in sheltered caves.

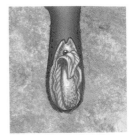

During the summer when their pools dry up, lungfish sleep in the mud. They use their lungs to breathe air.

Asleep in the soil

Just as some animals curl up and sleep all winter, bulbs are asleep, too, buried in the soil. They wait for the warm spring weather to come before they start to grow. See how a hyacinth bulb will not grow in the dark, but starts to grow shoots in the light.

Grow a bulb

1 Start this project in the fall. You will need a hyacinth bulb, a jar, and some toothpicks. Fill the jar nearly to the top with water.

2 Firmly stick four toothpicks in around the middle of the bulb. Balance the bulb in the top of the jar so its base is in the water.

3 Put the bulb in a dark closet. Check it occasionally to make sure it has enough water.

4 Before winter is over, bring the bulb out into the light. It will start to grow and you will soon have a beautifully scented hyacinth flower to enjoy.

Waiting to grow

Eggs, seeds, and tubers, such as potatoes, wait in the sand or earth until the weather is right for them to start to grow. While they are waiting, we say they are dormant.

Potatoes grow to their full size and then lie dormant underground until spring, when a new potato plant starts to grow.

Some mosquitos lay their eggs in mud. The larvae will not hatch until it rains and the mud becomes a pool for them to swim in.

Flower seeds can lie dormant in desert sands for a long time. They only grow when the rain comes.

Glossary

Air pressure
The air around and above you pushes down on you. This is called air pressure. Changes in air pressure usually bring changes in the weather.

Amphibians
Amphibians are animals such as newts that lay their eggs underwater. The young animals live underwater. The adults live both underwater and on land.

Barometer
A barometer is a device that measures air pressure. It can be used to predict the weather.

Bill
A bird's bill is its jaws. Each bird's bill is specially shaped for the kind of food it eats.

Camouflage
Camouflage is when the color and patterns on the coat or feathers of an animal or bird blend in with the background. This helps to keep them safe, as enemies cannot see them.

Carbohydrates
Carbohydrates in food give us energy and help us to keep going. They are found in foods like bread and pasta.

Carnivores
Carnivores are animals that eat meat. They hunt and kill other animals for food.

Cereals
Cereals are types of grasses, such as wheat, oats, rice, and corn, which are grown as crops. Cereals are a very important source of food for people and animals all over the world.

Chlorophyll
Chlorophyll is the green color in plants. Plants use chlorophyll to make food from sunlight.

Climate
The weather an area has throughout the year is called its climate.

Clouds

Clouds form when invisible water vapor in the air cools and turns into visible droplets of water.

Conifers

Conifers are evergreen trees that grow seeds in cones. Pine trees are conifers. They have long, thin leaves called needles.

Deciduous trees

Deciduous trees have large, flat leaves that change color in the fall, then fall off in winter. In the spring, fresh, green leaves grow.

Decomposers

Decomposers are creatures or plants that help dead animals and plants to break down, or decompose, in the soil.

Dormant

When plants are dormant, they are alive but have stopped growing. They wait until the weather is warm enough for them to grow again.

Egg

An egg is where new life starts. People and some animals keep eggs inside their bodies. Birds and fish lay their eggs. A bird's egg contains the food the young bird needs before it hatches.

Estivation

Estivation is a long, summer sleep that some animals have in parts of the world where there is very little water.

Evaporation

When a puddle of water dries up, the water itself does not disappear — it evaporates. This means that it turns into a gas, called water vapor.

Evergreen trees

Evergreen trees keep their leaves all year round. The leaves are often tough and shiny to protect them in cold weather.

Freshwater

Freshwater is the water we drink. Rainwater is fresh and so is most water found in rivers, ponds, and lakes.

Gravity

This is an invisible force that attracts objects to each other. The larger the object, the more gravity it has. The earth's gravity pulls everything down toward the ground.

Herbivores

Herbivores are animals that eat plants or parts of plants, such as nuts and berries. They are often eaten by carnivores.

Herbs

Herbs are plants that have a strong smell and taste in their stems and leaves. We use them for cooking, making herbal teas, and treating illnesses.

Hibernation

In the winter, when there is little food around, some animals save energy by going into a long sleep, called hibernation.

Metamorphosis

Metamorphosis is what happens to an animal that changes shape as it grows, such as a caterpillar changing into a butterfly.

Migration

Migration is the long journey that some creatures make in order to look for food.

Oxygen

Oxygen is an invisible gas in the air. It is very important because it lets all living things breathe and make energy.

Photosynthesis

Photosynthesis is when plants use sunlight, carbon dioxide, water, and the green color in their leaves, called chlorophyll, to make their own food.

Pollen

Pollen is the yellow dust inside a flower. Insects carry pollen from one flower to another.

Pollution

Pollution is when harmful chemicals escape into the air. It can cause nasty weather such as acid rain.

Proteins
Proteins help us grow and keep healthy. They are found in foods like meat and eggs.

Reproduction
For life to continue, all living things must make baby animals or new plants. This is called reproduction. Plants reproduce from seeds or another part of the plant. Animals reproduce when a seed from a male joins an egg from a female and a new life begins.

Reptiles
Reptiles are animals that lay eggs and have scaly, waterproof skin. Some live on land. Others, like crocodiles, live mainly in water.

Roots
Roots hold plants firmly in the ground. Water and minerals from the soil go up through the roots and into the plant.

Seawater
Seawater is salty because it contains minerals and salts that have been washed from the land into the sea.

Seeds
Plants grow from seeds. Inside a seed is a new plant and the food that it needs to begin to grow.

Temperature
Temperature is how warm or cold something is.

Thermometer
A thermometer is an instrument that is used for measuring temperature.

Tides
The sea moves backward and forward each day. These movements are called the tides.

Water vapor
Water vapor is the gas form of water. Most of the time it is invisible, but you can see it when water vapor cools and forms clouds.

Wind
Air that moves from one place to another is called wind. Winds can range from a gentle breeze to a whirling tornado.

Index

abdomen 75, 125
acid rain 28, 29
acorns 109, 118
air 9, 12, 14, 16, 21,
    28, 39, 40, 42, 51, 65,
    67, 71, 81, 94, 95,
    100, 103, 104, 137,
    151, 154, 156, 157
air pressure 14, 15,
    30, 154
amphibians 100, 154
antenna 75, 125
ants 56, 78, 79
aphids 91

backyard 4, 56–81, 134
badgers 105, 115
bark 109, 114
barometers 14, 15, 154
beans 92, 93
Beaufort Scale 13
bees 75, 85
beetles 75, 105, 109, 124
berries 71, 116, 145,
    156
bills 46, 47, 154
birds 46, 47, 49, 56,
    63, 70, 71, 72, 73,
    87, 98, 99, 106, 116,
117, 126, 127, 136,
    141, 143, 145, 148,
    149, 154, 155
bugs 75, 91, 124
bulbs 69, 97, 152, 153
butterflies 4, 75, 102,
    103, 124, 125, 140,
    141, 149, 156

camouflage 106, 126,
    127, 154
carbohydrates 90, 154
carbon dioxide 65, 156
carnivores 91, 104,
    105, 154, 156
caterpillars 71, 102,
    103, 109, 156
cereals 121, 154
chlorophyll 65, 146,
    154, 156
chrysalis 103
climate 8, 9, 10, 154
clouds 15, 16, 17, 18,
    31, 133, 155, 157
conifers 111, 117, 155
corn 120, 121, 154
countryside 64, 132
crocodiles 101, 157

deciduous trees 110,
    111, 112, 155
decomposers 61, 155
deer 73, 114, 115
deserts 9, 95
dormant 153, 155
dragonfly 40, 74, 103
droppings 63, 113, 114,
    128, 145

earth, the 6, 10, 11, 12,
    95, 104, 108, 156
eggs 40, 41, 45, 61, 68,
    69, 79, 86, 87, 98, 99,
    100, 101, 102, 103,
    105, 109, 116, 117,
    153, 154, 155, 157
embryo 86, 87
estivation 151, 155
evaporation 20, 21, 156
evergreen trees 110,
    111, 112, 117, 147,
    155

Fahrenheit 23, 31
fall 11, 111, 116, 118,
    130, 137, 144, 145,
    146, 148, 149, 150,
    152, 155
feathers 46, 98, 126,
    143, 154
ferns 113, 133
fish 39, 43, 47, 87,
    100, 155
fledgling 99
flour 120, 121
flowers 11, 58, 62, 68,
    69, 85, 93, 106,
    113, 122, 123, 124,
    136, 139, 140, 141,
    144, 153
footprints 4, 72, 73, 114
freshwater 35, 156
frogs 45, 100, 102, 137

fruit 63, 69, 72, 76, 90, 91, 144, 145

gills 43, 100
grains 120, 121
grasses 8, 63, 64, 65, 91, 120, 121, 122, 125, 126, 127, 129, 133, 136, 151, 154
grasshoppers 125, 136, 137
gravity 49, 156
grubs 109

hail 18, 19
hatching 87, 99, 101, 103, 105, 117, 153, 155
hatchling 101
herbivores 91, 104, 105, 156
herbs 134, 135, 156
hibernation 4, 150, 151, 156
holdfasts 50
holly 111, 147
horse chestnuts 63, 111, 118
hurricanes 27

ice 16, 17, 18, 19
insects 4, 32, 40, 46, 71, 74, 75, 76, 77, 78, 87, 93, 103, 106, 109, 116, 122, 124, 125, 126, 127, 135, 136, 149

ladybugs 75, 91
lakes 21, 34, 35, 156
larvae 105, 109, 153

leaves 4, 11, 13, 61, 65, 66, 67, 77, 80, 81, 91, 95, 97, 99, 102, 109, 110, 111, 112, 114, 117, 122, 123, 130, 132, 134, 135, 137, 138, 142, 143, 146, 147, 150, 151, 155, 156
legs 75, 77, 78, 100, 125, 129, 137
lichens 61, 113
life cycles 4, 82–105
lungs 43, 100, 151

maps 31, 56
mating 103, 137
meadows 106, 122–129
metamorphosis 102, 156
mice 73, 89, 115, 129
migration 130, 148, 149, 156
millipedes 76, 77
minerals 35, 58, 66, 67, 91, 157
moles 58, 128
moon, the 32, 49, 74
mosquito 39, 153
mosses 99, 113
moths 74, 140, 141

nectar 68, 93, 140, 141
needles 111, 132, 147, 155
nests 70, 78, 79, 87, 89, 98, 99, 116, 117, 126, 127, 128, 129, 137, 142
newts 100, 154
nuts 72, 109, 115, 116, 137, 156

oaks 109, 118, 133
oats 120, 121, 154
ovaries 68, 69, 85
oxygen 42, 43, 65, 156

pests 81, 125
petals 68, 122, 123, 138, 139
pheasants 132, 133
photosynthesis 65, 156
pines 111, 132, 147, 155
plants 4, 5, 8, 11, 35, 37, 38, 39, 40, 42, 44, 45, 50, 52, 58, 59, 60,

61, 62, 63, 65, 66, 67, 68, 74, 77, 80, 81, 82, 85, 86, 91, 92, 93, 94, 95, 96, 97, 100, 104, 105, 108, 113, 115, 130, 134, 138, 144, 153, 155, 156, 157
pollen 68, 69, 85, 156
pollution 28, 29, 41, 156
ponds 4, 32, 38, 39, 40, 41, 44, 45, 46, 137, 156
pondweed 42, 43, 44
protein 90, 157

rain 6, 9, 17, 18, 19, 20, 26, 30, 31, 34, 43, 44, 64, 77, 133, 135, 153, 156

rain forests 9, 95

reproduction 86, 87, 157

reptiles 100, 101, 157

rice 120, 121, 154

rivers 21, 32, 34, 35, 36, 37, 46, 156

rock pools 51, 52, 53

roots 50, 64, 67, 93, 95, 96, 97, 109, 157

salts 35, 91, 157

saltwater 35

scots pine 111, 118, 132, 133

seashore 32, 46, 50, 51, 142

seasons 6, 10, 11, 130, 136, 142

seaweed 48, 49, 50, 51

seeds 8, 46, 62, 63, 68, 69, 71, 85, 86, 87, 92, 93, 96, 115, 116, 117, 118, 119, 121, 123, 126, 127, 134, 138, 139, 144, 145, 153, 155, 157

sets, badger 115

shellfish 54, 55

shells 48, 54, 55, 86, 142

shoots 63, 93, 97, 139, 152

shrews 105

skins 100, 101, 103, 137, 157

slugs 76, 77

smog 28, 29

snails 39, 46, 71, 76, 77, 126

snakes 100, 101, 128

snow 6, 11, 17, 18, 19, 25, 34, 133

soil 5, 34, 35, 44, 45, 56, 58, 59, 60, 62, 64, 67, 74, 76, 80, 81, 94, 113, 118, 138, 152, 155

spawn 45, 100

sperm 87

spiders 76, 77

spring 11, 38, 70, 93, 98, 99, 112, 116,

118, 134, 136, 138, 144, 148, 149, 150, 152, 153

squirrels 115

stamen 68

sticklebacks 39

stigma 69, 85

storms 6, 12, 17, 26, 27, 31, 133

sugars 91

summer 11, 25, 38, 69, 116, 122, 125, 130, 134, 136, 138, 141, 146, 148, 151, 155

sun, the 5, 6, 10, 11, 15, 20, 21, 23, 24, 25, 49, 65, 103, 104, 139

sycamore 118

tadpoles 45, 100, 102

temperate regions 9

temperature 6, 22, 23, 25, 31, 133, 157

thermometer 22, 23, 24, 25, 30, 133, 157

thorax 75, 125

thunder and lightning 26, 31

tides 32, 48, 49, 52, 157

trees 11, 13, 27, 29, 62, 63, 91, 95, 98, 106, 108, 109, 110, 111, 112, 113, 114, 115, 116, 117, 118, 119, 127, 133, 137, 146, 147, 155

vitamins 90, 91

wasps 75, 109

water vapor 16, 17, 20, 21, 155, 157

weather 6–31, 93, 133, 150, 152, 153, 154, 155

weeds 62

wheat 120, 121, 154

wind 4, 6, 12, 13, 26, 27, 30, 31, 63, 64, 95, 123, 157

wings 40, 75, 103, 125, 137, 143

winter 9, 11, 25, 70, 71, 111, 116, 130, 137, 145, 147, 149, 150, 151, 152, 153, 155, 156

woodland 110–119

worms 49, 56, 58, 61, 71, 80, 81, 105, 126